WHAT

DO I DO

NOW?

A POWERFUL

LIFE CHANGING

BUSINESS SOLUTION

PHILIP PETERS
KATHLEEN PETERS

Published by National Information Services Corporation
P.O. Box 45
Canby, Oregon 97013
www.quantumabundancetheory.com

Cover design copyright 2011
by National Information Services Corporation.
Cover design by Georgann Gelsi-Piccirillo

ISBN: 978-0-615-50899-3

IN MEMORIAL
TO
R. SARGENT SHRIVER

On January 18, 2011 the world lost a great leader and humanitarian. R. Sargent Shriver, the first Director of the Peace Corps, the 21st United States Ambassador to France, and the first Director of the Office of Economic Opportunity was a tremendous positive influence on those of us who served with him in the early years of the Peace Corps.

His organizational skills, his compassion for the underprivileged, and his ebullient personality were all reflected down through the administrative ranks of the Peace Corps. For many of us the opportunity to meet him either during our service or afterward remains one of the outstanding events of our lives.

As I reached the end of my personal service with the Peace Corps I was privileged to receive from Sargent Shriver one of the 2,000 "Shriver Pins" that were given to those of us who served as Peace Corps Volunteers during the first years of its development. The small white pin with symbolically clasped green hands is a decoration that I have worn with pride down over the years. It now shall become, for me, a symbol of a life of service well lived.

DEDICATION

This book has been written as a joint

collaborative effort between Kathleen

and myself, just as we have developed the

large Wellness Marketing business that

we are privileged to operate.

Upon rare occasion two people will

come together and form a partnership

which transcends the normal relationships

between individuals. It is my privilege to

be able to share my vocation, my avocation,

my life and my Faith in God with the most

wonderful individual that I have ever known.

Thank you, Kathleen, for your Love,

your Understanding and your Patience.

DEDICATION

This book is dedicated to those who are praying,

searching and hoping for an answer..

This could be it.

INTRODUCTION

This story began to germinate in Kathleen's mind in the middle of a hurricane in Nova Scotia. Her thought was to develop a story that would relate the storms of life in the early Twenty-First Century to the difficulties of developing a true Social Entrepreneur business using the person-to-person Wellness Marketing business model.

As a Returned Peace Corps Volunteer Philip had for several years been toying with the idea of writing a story that would relate some of the challenges facing Returned Peace Corps Volunteers as they built their lives in the waning years of the Twentieth Century.

That night in Nova Scotia as the wind and rain battered the hotel where we were staying we began to bring the two stories together. It seemed plausible to create a novel about a Returned Peace Corps Volunteer who upon returning to the United States faced developing a life much broader in scope than had been imagined before that Volunteer had served two years overseas.

Combining Kathleen's twenty years of experience in the corporate world as a XEROX employee with Philip's experiences as a Peace Corps Volunteer and private businessman has proven to be a vehicle through which we could share some of our thoughts about life at the beginning of this new century.

John Fitzgerald Kennedy was elected President of the United States of America on Nov. 8, 1960. Within one year of that date the Peace Corps had been born and had begun recruiting Volunteers to serve two years overseas. For many of those who volunteered for those first projects, the 1950's had been an idyllic time to grow up. The undercurrents of racial tension, class struggle and the changes in sexual values that would take place over the next decade were for the most part hardly visible to many of those first Volunteers.

The U.S. economy was growing robustly and even with the periodic downturns no one among those mostly youthful adventurers foresaw the huge changes that would come about as we entered the Twenty-First Century.

The abrupt and painful death of President Kennedy on November 23, 1963 in Dallas, Texas not only had an everlasting effect on each of those who served under him in those first months of the Peace Corps but also began to change forever the tone and tenor of the people of the United States. Luke, the main character, is a Returned Peace Corps Volunteer who has been forced by circumstances beyond his control to live through many of the real life experiences of the "Baby Boomers" of the early Twenty-First Century. At one point, after having developed a very comfortable lifestyle, Luke realizes that the dense jungle of Guatemala is very similar in many ways to the dilemmas facing people today who are attempting to find their way through the dense jungle of Twenty-First Century life struggles.

The Peace Corps group that Luke is a part of (Guatemala I) was real. Philip served in Guatemala with that group. In 1962, the group actually did part of its' training in Puerto Rico and part of it at New Mexico State University. If some of you from Guatemala I should read this novel you may recognize an incident or certain characteristics of persons in the book. There has been no attempt to create characters anything like any of the former Peace Corps Volunteers in Guatemala I. The man described as "El Aleman" was a man of mystery and his periodic visits to Tierra Fuerte really did take place in the town that was Philip's assigned site. Tierra Fuerte, however, is itself not a real town. Cesar, the principal of the school in the fictional Tierra Fuerte, was a real life principal and friend of Philip's. In

8

1963 Cesar and Philip did build a clinic in their real town much as is described and Cesar was very important to the successful completion of that project.

Obviously, Sargent Shriver, as the first Director of The Peace Corps, was a very real person and a man whom Philip continues to hold in the highest esteem.

As Luke returns to the USA and then develops his life at home we have put in vignettes, thoughts and ideas that have been expressed to us over the years by many Returned Peace Corps Volunteers, as well as others who have been faced with the life challenges of the last decades. The struggles that Luke goes through when he is downsized and then eventually finds a gainful way in which to create a substantial income are all based on real incidents that many people in the United States have experienced in the time period from about 2003 through today. Sadly, many people continue to experience these challenges in their everyday lives.

Tom Simon is a composite of several people we have known who all believe strongly that we, as unique human personalities, in many ways determine our own destinies.

The Wellness Revolution and the resultant Wellness Industry are very real and are literally changing today's world. Philip and Kathleen are very actively involved in building their own large international business in this industry. When Philip himself first entered the Natural Food and Medicine Industry as a product manufacturer in the 1960's it was estimated that only about 2% of the American people admitted to having been inside a health food store. Chiropractic Medicine and Acupuncture were regarded as "non-medical" types of treatment practices and often had been referred to as "quackery." In this first decade of the Twenty-First Century it is estimated that 75% of the U.S. population participate in some type of alternative medicine program and use natural foods and medicines in their own home. Chiropractic Medicine, Acupuncture and a host of other complimentary medicine practices are now recognized and implemented by major hospitals, care centers and medical doctors across the entire globe. Major medical schools now include as a part of their regular curriculum studies in glycobiology, and nutrition.

In the wake of the financial breakdown of the first decade of the Twenty-First Century and the publicly exposed abuses by leading financiers of the day a new method of doing business is springing forth.

The day of the Social Entrepreneur is upon us! Business schools across the nation are teaching classes in entrepreneurship as a means of helping put people back to work. Companies such as Tom's Shoes, Starbucks and Mannatech are stepping forward to change both the practice and culture of business. In many cases these organizations and companies are being led or influenced by former Peace Corps Volunteers like John Hatch, the founder of FINCA and its worldwide village banking programs.

The term "Social Entrepreneur" is relatively new in usage. It describes a new generation of entrepreneurial change makers who refuse to accept the status quo of poverty, disease and hunger throughout the world. To solve these problems requires the radical growth and change of business and marketing. These individuals, male and female, from all the continents of the globe do not fit a common mold. But, they do often have many of the same characteristics. They tend to be energetic, compassionate, creative, impatient, driven by passion and focused on resolving what has become for them a specific major problem of the world or a given culture. Tied to this is most often the desire to provide a product or service to the estimated four billion low income consumers across the world. Profit is often a motive as their companies and efforts grow but they tend to view profit as a service vehicle rather than an end in itself. At the same time that a product or service is being provided it also often serves to provide an increased source or method of income for impoverished peoples.

Social entrepreneurs are not new. The term is new. But in today's world of conflict, terrorism and fear the social entrepreneur stands to be the change agent that hopefully will move civilization worldwide to a new and higher level of cooperation and concern for each other.

Through this work of fiction it has been our desire to show you, the reader, how one or two individuals through helping others to have a comfortable lifestyle can be of great service and aid to many who are less fortunate.

For Philip, the Peace Corps was his first step in this growth pattern. For Kathleen, her introduction to the corporate world of XEROX broadened her views of corporate responsibility. We give you this book in the hope that it may serve as a step on your personal path to developing a substantial personal income and a vehicle for public service

A special thanks must be given to Philip's brother, Clark Peters, who was the first person to critically review this work for us. We wish also to give special thanks to Sam Caster, Co-Founder of MannaRelief Ministries for taking his valuable time to review our manuscript and give us his objective comments. This book would have been much more difficult to publish had it not been for the graphic and organizational talents of Georgann Gelsi-Piccirillo. There were several who assisted us in different ways as we wrote this novel; Jim Mallen, Rev. Jeffrey Leininger, Nancy Leininger, Dewey Hayes, and Larry Lundgren, to only name a few. We thank you all. We give special thanks to our children for their encouragement and input on this project.

It is our most sincere hope that through this novel we can share with you a certain amount of wisdom that has been given to us over the years and that it will be helpful to you, the reader.

Philip Peters   Kathleen Peters

CHAPTER ONE

*"Ask not what your country can
do for you. Ask what you can do
for your country."*

John Fitzgerald Kennedy

Fifty years! Five decades! How had time passed so quickly? Luke glanced at the letter which lay beside him on the little table that he and his wife, Kathryn, used when they would sit here on the porch in the late afternoon and enjoy the quiet and a glass of wine. The letter had been delivered to their home outside Portland, Oregon last week before they came down to their "get away" home for the week. The return address read National Peace Corps Association. The letter itself was an invitation to attend the Fiftieth Anniversary of the Peace Corps which was to be held on September 22-25, 2011 in Washington, D.C.

Luke had come out on the porch this afternoon to smoke his pipe and relax. He loved this secluded retreat he had purchased many years ago, even before he was out of college, for just this very purpose. In many ways it had become for him and Kathryn the most romantic and idyllic spot they could have ever imagined. Nestled among the Douglas Fir trees on the south side of the Nehalem River about fifteen miles east of Seaside, Oregon he had known the instant he first saw it that he would buy it to enjoy someday with his future family. After he and Kathryn were married they had always called it the "beach house" even though, in reality, it was miles from the closest beach.

Built of logs by a Portland architect it had originally been four bedrooms with a beautiful stone fireplace in the huge front room. The porch he was sitting on now faced the Nehalem River about two hundred feet away down a grassy bank. The river was far enough away and sufficiently lower than the house that even in the worst flood years the water had never come close to them. Over the years they had planted a grassy lawn and put in azaleas, rhododendrons, iris flowers and evergreen bushes so that the area between the house and the river was like a small botanical park. A few years ago Luke had spent most of one summer putting in a small secluded area on the east side of the lawn with a pond about eight feet across which he had stocked with goldfish. Fortunately they were down out of the mountains of the Coast Range where it seldom snowed and did not freeze. He had placed a carved wooden bench on the east side facing toward the west so they could sit and watch the sun set into the hills that lay between them and the ocean. He had hauled several pick-up loads of rock down from an abandoned quarry, originally developed when the highway department built the Sunset Highway across the mountains from Portland to Seaside years before. He had used the rock to create small pockets around the edges of the lawn where each spring Kathryn planted colorful perennials and annuals that grew into a beautiful outdoor bouquet all summer long. For Luke and Kathryn it was the most perfect place in the world to get away from their hectic life back at their "real" home in the Willamette Valley.

They had driven down yesterday because this weekend was their annual family reunion and party. They had started the tradition when their two oldest boys were still only toddlers. Their family eventually had grown to four children and when they arrived later today and tomorrow with all the wives, husbands and grandchildren it would become bedlam! But they all loved the time together and Luke and Kathryn looked forward to it each summer.

Luke glanced again at the envelope. How could the Peace Corps possibly be fifty years old? He had joined as a Volunteer in

1962 and had been assigned to what became known as Guatemala I. Luke settled deeper into his favorite chair, lit his pipe and his mind drifted back over the years just as his pipe smoke was drifting lazily up past the eaves.

He had been twenty-four years old and fresh out of Oregon State University when he had met a Peace Corps recruiter at the Portland State College Bookstore in downtown Portland, Oregon. The man was there to give a talk later in the afternoon and he invited Luke to attend. They had talked briefly, just enough to pique Luke's curiosity and then they parted. That afternoon Luke sat in the back of a classroom and listened as the recruiter talked about President Kennedy and what he and his brother-in-law Sargent Shriver, as Director of the Peace Corps, intended for the Peace Corps to become over the next decade. Luke had always wanted to travel and did not even have a steady girlfriend at the time. The more he listened the more fascinated he became. At the end of the presentation several people had questions but many of them filed out rather quickly.

Most of the people were gone when Luke walked up to the front of the room and began to question the speaker. As the questions became more direct and personal Luke suddenly had asked, "Are you doing anything this evening? Why don't we go have dinner?" The man had agreed and they had gone downtown to The New Republic, one of Luke's favorite Chinese restaurants, and had talked for nearly three hours over Chinese food and tea. By the time they had finished, Luke knew that he was going to apply to become a Peace Corps Volunteer. The recruiter gave him all the necessary papers and before he went to bed that night he had filled them out and had them ready to mail in the morning. As he had lain back in the darkness with his hands folded behind his head he knew with a certainty he had seldom felt that his life and world were changing. Somehow he had changed in only a matter of hours. He knew the steps he had just taken were the first steps on a journey to become the man he had always dreamed of being. As he drifted off to sleep visions of adventure and grand exploration played through his mind.

Somehow he had known that he would be accepted. The recruiter had suggested to him that with his background of having grown up on a farm and the fact he already had a college degree, even though it was a Forestry Management degree, he might well be accepted into a rural Peace Corps program.

It seemed to Luke it took forever to hear anything back from his application. But, one day in the mail there was a letter asking him to call a number in Washington, D.C. and speak with a person doing oral interviews over the telephone. The next day Luke called and for nearly an hour talked with a young woman over the phone who seemed to be trying to convince Luke that if he were accepted he would definitely enjoy his two years as a Volunteer. Luke had been slightly amused at the conversation because she did not seem to understand she did not need to convince him and he was just waiting for word that he was being accepted.

Again he waited for what seemed to be a terribly long time. But one afternoon there in the mail was a white envelope with a blue Peace Corps return address on it. Luke had torn open the envelope and indeed it was an invitation to join a Community Development group being formed to serve in Guatemala. He chuckled to himself as he remembered he had to go to his world globe to find Guatemala and be sure where it really was. The letter told him he was to be in New York City on November 22, 1962 to meet his group and fly to Puerto Rico for the first month of his training.

Luke had told his mother and father that night at their home what he was doing. His father had quietly smiled and had been supportive of his decision. His mother had been much different. She had expressed her concerns for his safety and the fact that for two years he would not be with her for Mother's Day, Christmas and the other family gatherings. His father had quietly told her this was Luke's decision, not theirs, and his mother had turned to him with a hug and agreed she thought it was a great opportunity. The next few weeks flew by as he arranged for his Passport, got the required medical forms completed, obtained the proper World Health Organization card and what seemed like a million other things he had to do before he left.

Luke had never traveled outside the United States before and he eagerly boarded his flight to New York and what was to be a two year life-changing adventure for him.

Being a young man in very good physical shape Luke found the Puerto Rico training experience both rigorous and at times amusing. There were two training camps used by the Peace Corps near the town of Arecibo in Puerto Rico and the camp Luke was assigned to was Camp Crozier named after a Peace Corps Volunteer who had died the year before while on assignment in South America. For Luke the most difficult challenge had been the language training. Their first day in Camp Crozier they were divided into groups of about eight Volunteers each according to their ability to speak Spanish and sent to bunkhouses that would become their classrooms. One of the most beautiful Spanish women he had ever seen walked into the room. She wrote on the blackboard, "No English! I am married!" and started their class by holding up a pen and saying, "La pluma." They soon understood they were to repeat after her and this began their total immersion in their language training program. Little did Luke realize how much he would use the Spanish language she taught them!

Luke had grown up in the Pacific Northwest and was accustomed to the green trees that grew there year round, but Puerto Rico was totally different than anything he had ever experienced before. The lush foliage was a hundred different shades of green. The varieties of flowers that ranged from bright scarlet red through orange to the yellow of the sun constantly amazed him. The one thing that he first noticed in Puerto Rico that he would realize many times in later life was the heavily humid smell of the tropics. It was a strange delightfully oppressive scent that he always would find very difficult to describe. The flowers had beautiful bouquet scents that were sweet and almost fruity but that aroma always joined with an underlying odor of decay and earthiness which created an oddly strange scent that existed only in the tropics. It was a scent that worked its way permanently into your senses so that when you thought of the jungle you always thought of that one distinctive smell.

Luke never quite understood if Camp Crozier had been built just for their training or if it had actually existed earlier for some other perhaps more clandestine type training. The facilities were basically very simple. Men and women were separated in bunkhouse type plain wooden buildings. Everything was built to be open and airy wherever possible.

One of the most interesting activities that took place during that month in Puerto Rico had been the overnight experience that each Trainee was required to spend out in the jungle by him or herself.

Fortunately for Luke he had hunted and fished all his life and had been out in the Northwest forests many times by himself. Even with that background he had thought that the dense, dark jungle was quite different from the forests of the Northwest.

Each Trainee was given a map, a compass, a "C" ration pack, a canteen with water, matches and a blanket. The Trainees were told they would be dropped off at intervals along a faint jungle trail where they would be spending the night by themselves. The night out would end the following morning and they would meet back together at a certain time at a location marked with a red "X" on the map.

Luke had actually enjoyed the time by himself and except for the ever present jungle insects it would have been a very enjoyable experience. That night he had wondered how the people who had never been by themselves in an isolated location would fare. He especially wondered about some of the young women who had spent most of their lives in cities. For some of them this must be a very frightening time.

That evening he took the opportunity to explore around his assigned site and he even found a large anthill with little columns of ants marching in and out. It was fascinating to watch the way one column marched in laden down with twigs, leaves and fibers and another column a few inches away marched out empty handed to search around the mound for leaves and vegetation to carry back into their home. That night he heard birds talking to each other several times. In the early morning he heard what he thought might have been a monkey.

Only once had he been concerned about his safety. About one o'clock in the morning he heard an animal moving around his little camp area and he knew from the sounds that it was a fairly large animal. Being in a totally strange area, having no weapon for defense, and not knowing what kind of animals might be wild in this jungle he had thrown a rock out into the heavy foliage in the direction of the sound. After that he heard nothing else until he was awakened by the birds at dawn.

He had smuggled a little packet of instant coffee, creamer and sugar out of the mess hall at lunch the day before and he lit a small fire and heated the water in his canteen to make himself a drink of morning coffee. Not having to be at the assigned location on the map for a couple of hours he continued his exploration of the night before. The leaves were broad and heavy on most of the plants and he was sure that some of the plants growing close by were taro plants. The trees were tall and he was surprised that even though the cover from the tree boughs and branches was quite dense there were many types of small green leafy plants growing on the jungle floor. The air was still cool from the night and the sun was barely peeking through the leafy cover high above as Luke sat on a log and enjoyed the fabulous beauty of the jungle morning. The beauty seemed to be accentuated in a vacuum of total quiet. A few birds could be heard but no other jungle sounds broke into his silent enjoyment.

At the appointed time all the Trainees had gathered except for one girl who Luke had thought looked to be about twenty years old at the most. The drivers of the two carry-alls sent to pick them up finished the coffee they had brought with them and were about to leave when she pushed her way out of the jungle growth and stepped onto the gravel road. She had a very sullen look on her face and with hardly a word to anyone she climbed into the back of one of the vehicles and they headed for camp.

Later that day Luke heard that she and one other young woman had asked to be taken back to San Juan so that they could return home.

The month of December flew by and before he knew it he was on a flight back to Portland with orders to report to New Mexico State University in Las Cruces, New Mexico right after the New Years holiday for a three month training program in Community Development.

Returning to Portland at Christmas time was a perfect break for Luke. He had always loved the Holidays in "River City" as many locals called Portland because of the Willamette River which ran through the center of town. He was going to be home for two weeks and perhaps during that time he would be able to do some Christmas shopping at Saturday Market. Created as a street market under one of the many bridges that crossed the Willamette River, Saturday Market was becoming home to local vendors of Oregon produced gift items, artwork and an amazing variety of foods. Luke especially enjoyed getting a cup of coffee and finding a seat near the old Skidmore Fountain where he could enjoy watching the children playing. Amateur jugglers, musicians and other entertainers were always gathered there in the hope that someone would share a few coins with them.

He had done exactly that this morning and as he finished his coffee he wandered up the side streets of downtown until he realized that he was across the street from the Meier and Frank Department Store. The venerable old store had developed the tradition many years before of every Christmas decorating each of the large street level display windows with a Christmas story. As he looked in a corner window he realized that this year they had used a special Fairy Tale Christmas theme. He might as well walk all the way around the block square store and look at all the windows.

Each of the windows this year told a separate story from a children's fairy tale. One corner window even had live animals in it to make the story more real. At this corner window a large group of children and adults stood watching the rabbits, goats, sheep and birds that were a part of that windows story. As he stood watching the small children crowding up to the window he saw that they even had a small burro in a stable toward the back of the large display. The final window contained several human size wooden nutcrackers and music from The Nutcracker Suite flooded the sidewalk from speakers up under the eaves.

His two week "leave" period passed far too quickly and before he hardly realized it he was on a plane headed for New Mexico and the next phase of his training.

The three months at New Mexico State were filled with memorable events of all types but most memorable of all was the process used for selecting which Volunteers would actually go to Guatemala. They were all given to understand at the beginning of the program that each week there would probably be some who would be selected "out" and they would simply leave with no good byes. The first time this happened there were simply three faces not in class one morning and everyone understood they had been sent home during the night. More than half of the group that started in New York had been "selected out" by the time they were ready to leave for Guatemala. The twenty-seven men and women who arrived in Guatemala City in March of 1963 were confident they were going to be able to assist the local Guatemalans they would be working with to improve their lives and that overall they would somehow be making a contribution to world peace.

Luke realized his pipe had gone out and thinking considerable time had passed he looked at his watch only to realize that just twenty minutes had slipped by. His reverie about Puerto Rico had brought back many memories he had not thought of for years. He heard the rattle of pans in the kitchen as Kathryn prepared food ahead for tomorrows meals and he thought of how many celebrations had taken place here on the bank of the river. Birthdays, anniversaries, one of their daughters had even been married on the lawn down by the river.

As he thought about the memories of past events here in this yard his gaze settled on the hammock hanging on the porch just a few feet away. He stood up and stretched. Moving the small table over to where he could reach it from the hammock he settled down into it and pulled on the rope he had hung from a beam so whoever was in the hammock could gently swing it simply by pulling on the rope. How many evenings had he and Kathryn stretched out side by side in this hammock and quietly talked about the children, their own dreams, and their love for each other? Those were truly among the most enjoyable times of his life, when he could feel her soft and warm beside him and they could gently talk to each other. He chuckled to himself as he thought of how many times in the middle of some husband/wife argument one of them had taken the other by the hand and led the way to the hammock. They both knew there was to be no arguing in the hammock and many spirited discussions had been slowed to gentle touches as they lay and listened to the river at the bottom of the slope.

Kathryn had always enjoyed having the hammock and it had become especially comfortable for her after he had explained that this very hammock had hung outside his room in Guatemala and how often he had gone out to lie in it and let its gentle sway ease his mind away from the cares of his days there. He had cared for it well and even though it was old in years it remained strong and able to support both of them. So many things had taken place in the fifty plus years that he had owned this home. How did all of this and all of the things that had happened to him in the last fifty years relate to those experiences half a century ago that had reshaped his goals, his desires and yes, his life forever? He recalled how throughout their training they had been told over and over in a hundred different ways, that their two years as Peace Corps Volunteers would have an impact on the lives of their host-country people they worked with, but that one of the most important aspects of their two years would be the increased knowledge, understanding and cultural appreciation they would bring back from Guatemala when they returned to the United States and began to develop their new post Peace Corps activities.

How true that had been. No Returned Peace Corps Volunteer had yet served as President of the United States but as Luke let his mind drift he thought of U.S. Senators, Members of the House of Representatives, high government officials, business leaders, local politicians, and religious leaders who had first served as Peace Corps Volunteers and then upon their return to the U.S. had developed lives and roles of importance and influence. Look at how it had affected his own life.

Guatemala I had been a Community Development Project and the Volunteers had been scattered miles apart all across the country mostly in remote areas. He had been stationed in a small village called Tierra Fuerte about thirty miles into the mountains from the capital, Guatemala City. The village was an interesting conglomeration of ancient Indian traditions and the newer Spanish influences. He had also found that the Twentieth Century had definitely affected village life.

They had arrived in Guatemala City directly from New Mexico and each of the following fourteen days had been full of a variety of activities. They had traveled by bus from the airport in Guatemala City to the ancient capital of Antigua. Each of them had met their local counterparts who all worked for the Guatemalan Agricultural Extension Agency which was named Instituto Agropecuario Nacional (IAN).

Antigua itself was an old Spanish city with many churches and government buildings that had been destroyed over the centuries by earthquakes. They had taken several very interesting field trips that were led by a local historian, a minor government official and a very lovely Guatemalan woman who lived in a nearby village. The native people they were meeting seemed to range all the way from a small group who represented themselves to be of pure Mayan/Quiche Indian background through to the largest group formed by the Spanish who had settled in this area intermingling with the ancient Indian peoples. The smallest and most well educated group was made up of a very few descendants of the early Spaniards, some Germans who had settled throughout Latin America in the early Twentieth Century and an assortment of other Europeans. Luke would later learn that often in the remotest villages he would also find an isolated person of Chinese heritage who owned the local tienda or store.

Some of the most beautiful people Luke would ever meet were men and women made up of the intermingling of the Europeans and the Indians. With striking copper hued skin, coal black hair, and black eyes which were very difficult to read, they were usually well muscled with finely developed physiques.

Many of the churches and other buildings in the area had never been rebuilt after they had fallen to earthquakes in the years of the Spanish occupation. One church, right in Antigua, had been destroyed in about 1650 and even though the four walls still stood it was totally unsafe for reconstruction. Built of stone, adobe, timber and mud it had apparently been quite large and of great importance. Hundreds of years later even a portion of the original stone altar still existed. The Trainees had been taken down about a dozen steps to a dark, cool underground crypt as the guide explained about the Spaniard who had originally been buried there.

As they traveled to Tierra Fuerte from Antigua they passed Indians walking in both directions going about their many and varied activities. The clothing they wore was often very colorful and the colors and patterns were how each person knew automatically where the other person was from geographically. Each region or village had developed over the generations its own colorful pattern or weave that defined, even better than a written placard, where the wearer was from.

The Guatemalan jungle on the road from Antigua down to Tierra Fuerte on the Pacific Coast was denser and, if possible, had even more brightly colored flowers than he had seen on the roads in Puerto Rico.

The closer they got to Tierra Fuerte, which was well up on the side of the mountains but still low enough to be very tropical in appearance, the more wild banana trees they saw. The foliage, the bushes and the vines along the sides of the road were heavy and thick. Periodically they would pass a small clearing with from one to perhaps four small houses built of sticks and woven vines or branches. Even though having a primitive appearance they seemed to be quite strong and well built. Little children, usually naked, played in the clearings and would stop to watch their light blue carry-all type vehicle if it slowed or honked at an animal in the road.

The jungle hues of green were intense and varied. The mingled smell of flowers, dust, and vegetation were so intense that at times they seemed to overwhelm him. Luke was alive with anticipation and with the excitement of finally being close to where he would be living and working for the next two years.

CHAPTER TWO

"Two roads diverged in a wood,
and I took the one less traveled by,
And that has made all the difference."

The Road Not Taken
Robert Frost

One afternoon after having been in Tierra Fuerte several weeks Luke had been at the small one room Post Office when an old but well polished Mercedes Benz had stopped outside the front door. An obviously Spanish man who had been driving came in and asked for mail from the wizened and aged Indian who served as Postmaster for the village. As he put the mail into a small canvas bag he glanced once at Luke. With no greeting, no smile and seemingly no interest he turned and went out to the car. The window rolled down on the back door on the driver's side and he handed the mailbag through to a heavy older man's white hand that took the bag and then the window was closed. As the Mercedes pulled away Luke asked a friend of his who was in the car. His friend gave him the only answer he would ever receive about the man's identity. "El Aleman." For the two years that Luke lived in the village, each week the heavy Mercedes Benz would pull up to the Post Office, the Spaniard would get out, get the mail and hand it through the back window. Luke never learned who the man was but one day in a local newspaper from Guatemala City he read an article buried in the middle section of the paper about World War II Germans who were living out their lives in exile to avoid the war crimes tribunals. As the months went by and Luke explored the mountains around Tierra Fuerte he happened to drive up a curving rocky road that curled past a cement house set well back from the road surrounded by a heavy wrought iron fence. The gate was closed and securely locked. There was no sign of any living person on the grounds. Later in the day after he had returned to the village Luke asked at the local tienda who lived in the cement house up on the mountain. Again the answer was simply, "El Aleman."

Luke had expected he might work with some type of forestry project but the local Agricultural Extension Agency had no forestry projects of any type for him to work with for his entire stay in Tierra Fuerte. Luke was later to learn that many Volunteers assigned to Community Development Projects were at a loss as to what they were really supposed to accomplish. As the weeks began to slow down and boredom from lack of a specific project began to wear on him Luke became well acquainted with the local school "principal." Cesar was his name and he had graduated from high school in Guatemala City four years before Luke arrived. There was a female teacher at the school also who had graduated from college in the Capitol but because Cesar had been a teacher first he was appointed principal.

One night as Luke and Cesar sat in the tienda drinking their second liter of Gallo Cervesa Luke asked Cesar what the town truly needed the most. Two hours and another liter of Gallo apiece later, Luke and Cesar had agreed that what Tierra Fuerte needed more than anything else was a medical clinic.

With over five hundred people living in and close by the village there was no medical service available without going clear to Guatemala City which often was a full days trip by bus.

Over the next six months with the help of the Guatemalan National Department of Education, the Multnomah County Medical Society, CARE, an unexpected financial donor and the United States Embassy in Guatemala City, Luke and Cesar were able to build a simple two room clinic and supply it with basic equipment and supplies.

Cesar had personally carved from wood a Quetzal bird to place over the door of the clinic. Cesar's family was descended from the family of the great Quiche Indian, Tecun Uman who had been the leader of the last Maya-Quiche battles against the Spanish Conquistadores. Killed in the highlands of Guatemala by the Spanish leader Pedro de Alvorado in 1524 Tecun Uman had quickly become a national hero. The Quetzal bird had been Tecun Uman's constant companion. Even living with him in his headdress. Upon Tecun Uman's death the bird had flown his own body, soaked with Tecun Uman's blood, away from Tecun Uman and into the jungle where, according to Mayan legend, the Quetzal never sang again. Living in the jungles the bird was rarely seen but from the time of Tecun Uman's death onward the bird's bright green plumage was marked by a blood red breast.

Only once, when Cesar had taken Luke deep into the jungle and they had sat quietly for several hours, had Luke actually seen the beautiful long tailed Quetzal in the wild. It was a sight that he had never forgotten and which had even become a part of his own spiritual quest to better understand life around him.

The first day the clinic was open, staffed by volunteer Medical Doctors and Nurses from Roosevelt Hospital in Guatemala City, they had seen over one hundred patients. When Luke left Guatemala to return home after completing his Peace Corps service the clinic was seeing an average of seven hundred patients every weekend. Luke remembered that clinic every time he thought of his village home in Guatemala.

The day he left the village to return to the Capitol for his post service evaluations before returning to the United States he knew he had made the contribution he was meant to make.

He had returned home from Guatemala in 1965 unsure of whether he wanted to immediately get a job or return to school for an advanced degree. When Sargent Shriver, as the first Director of the Peace Corps, had personally presented them with "Shriver pins" as part of the first two thousand Volunteers to have completed service he had made the point that they would probably be very unsettled as to exactly what career path they would want to follow. That afternoon, as Luke had shaken hands with this man who had formed and molded the Peace Corps for President Kennedy, he had been humbled by the overwhelming feeling that he had truly been involved in a great movement. Shriver's personal contact with the Volunteers, even to the point of mentioning the clinic in Tierra Fuerte, was one of the characteristics of the man that Luke admired. Luke had always been proud to wear the little white pin with the symbolic green hands clasped and he had even heard the rumor that Shriver himself had been instrumental in designing the pin.

If Luke looked for a job what did he really want that to be? He knew that he did not want to teach in elementary or high school. He also knew that he wanted to do something that would make a contribution to society and provide a substantial income so he could provide well for a future family. Was there some aspect of a social work career that would serve his purpose? He didn't think he could make enough money in that field so he put it off to one side. Luke began to look at possible universities he might attend that would help to strengthen his career opportunities. He even began to fill out admission forms.

He had formed a small consulting company after his return to do some work in forestry but still wasn't sure that was where he belonged. Then one day out of the blue came a phone call. The man on the other end introduced himself as being a representative of a new program starting in Washington, D.C. as a part of President Lyndon Johnson's *War on Poverty*.

"I understand that you served in Guatemala in the Peace Corps and that you speak Spanish. Is that correct?" Luke agreed and the voice on the phone continued, "Could we have coffee tomorrow in Portland? I am going to be here for about five days and I am hiring staff for our new offices."

Sargent Shriver had been appointed Director of the new Office of Economic Opportunity (OEO) and when Luke heard that he immediately listened carefully to what the man had to say.

Even though his experience had been that many Volunteers assigned to Community Development Projects were often at a loss as to what their actual job activity was to be he had been extremely impressed with the way Shriver had organized the Peace Corps and anticipated that OEO would be run much the same way. Luke had been drawn as a Peace Corps Volunteer to Shriver's ebullient personality and his abundant creative energy which had made him, in Luke's opinion, one of President Kennedy's most successful leaders.

That phone call had set Luke on a path that over the next ten years would see him become a professional trainer, and an accomplished public speaker which would develop for him a broad range of political contacts. It also led him to what would become his major career activity in the timber industry. Had anyone attempted to tell him in 1962 that by becoming a Peace Corps Volunteer he would be opening the door to both a political consulting career and one in the international timber industry he would have scoffed at their wild thoughts.

But as he sat here on the Nehalem River thinking about how his life had unfolded he realized that virtually every one of the major events could be traced back to some type of influence that had come out of those two years. One major event in his life that had not grown out of his two years as a Peace Corps Volunteer had been Kathryn's entrance into it.

CHAPTER THREE

"Tell everyone what you want to do
and someone will want to help you do it."

W. Clement Stone

"Meet me under the clock in the Meier and Frank Department Store." his brother Mark had said when they had agreed to have lunch together at noon that day four decades past. His brother was always prompt but today for some reason it was already twenty past twelve and there was no sign of him. Waiting had been fine with Luke because he had always enjoyed "people watching." It was always busy at noon here in the center of the first floor of the old downtown Portland department store. An older woman with her granddaughter moved around him to look closer at a piece of costume jewelry on a polished display case. His eyes wandered around the floor noting the way people laughed, frowned or showed no emotion at all. As his gaze came to the escalator he could not help but notice the attractive ankles in sheer black stockings and black high heels coming down the moving stairway. His eyes traveled up to the most incredibly beautiful face he had ever seen. Striking olive eyes set beneath arched black eyebrows framed the eyes so that they truly were "windows into the soul." Rich, coal black hair fell around her face and shoulders so that her creamy white skin made the entire vision seem to be a framed oil painting. This face, that hair, those eyes were the very face and eyes he had seen in his dreams a thousand different times. How could this possibly be? Even as those thoughts were tumbling through his mind he realized she was smiling directly at him. Then she was off the escalator and with a saucy sway was moving away through the crowd. At six feet tall Luke was tall enough to see that black mane moving away but knew of no reasonable way to call out to her. Then she was gone behind a counter piled high with men's dress shirts. As she disappeared Luke could recall everything about her. She was wearing a black silk blouse tucked into a soft gray skirt that stopped right at her knees. She had been wearing a strand of pearls that hung down around her throat and emphasized the beauty of her neckline. Even though she had not spoken a word he could hear the sound of her laughter and the softly strong timbre of her voice. What was he doing standing here daydreaming about a woman he had only seen for ten seconds at the most! And yet, deep within him he knew he had seen her before.

Later that same evening, after returning home from lunch with Mark, as he sat on his front porch looking out over the narrow Nehalem River in front of his ranch style log house he sucked on his pipe and as the smoke curled around his head he remembered how truly beautiful she had been coming down the escalator. He had always liked and enjoyed good looking women. Fortunately for him they seemed to find him attractive also and that had led him to a number of relationships over his twenty-eight years. But never had he encountered in real life the woman he first knew as his "Gypsy Queen" in his dreams when he was in the eighth grade. From those early years Luke had always dreamt about this same vision. He had never fully accepted the idea that somehow he had a foresight or vision of his future partner and spouse, yet unconsciously he had in high school, college and as a Peace Corps Volunteer compared every girl or woman he dated to this shadow person who was always in his mind. Since that first dream years ago she had grown in his mind to be beautiful, sensual, intellectually amazing and perfectly suited to his particular lifestyle. As his pipe began to burn low and the coolness from the river soaked into his shirt his thoughts had turned to other matters which had him greatly concerned. He was going to have to do something other than just the consulting business he had set up for himself when he returned to the U.S. from Guatemala.

In his silent thoughts later as he lay in bed letting his body relax for sleep he recalled again and again that lovely black hair and those amazing eyes.

He very seldom dreamt but as he awakened in the morning he had the strange feeling that he had dreamt about the woman on the escalator and with the dream had been a message to the effect that he would meet her if he would only go out and search for her. Dressing casually for the day he had taken his morning coffee out onto the porch to listen to the river and the waking birds.

Luke had always been an avid reader and for all of his life he had been accustomed to the presence of books. That morning as his coffee sat and cooled his eyes had settled upon a book he had purchased when he lived in Guatemala and had hardly opened. The title for some reason had attracted his attention, THINK AND GROW RICH. The author was someone named Napoleon Hill with whom he was unfamiliar. But the title had seemed to jump at him off the bookshelf in the bookstore.

Peggy, his Peace Corps partner in Tierra Fuerte, Guatemala had claimed she had insightful intuitive abilities. For certain, he had seen her on several occasions be correct in regard to opinions she had about his acquaintances. She had said to him one evening as they sat drinking coffee at the pension in the village where they lived that she believed there were no coincidences in life and that virtually everything happening in our lives has a purpose. He had chuckled at her with the wisdom of a young recent college graduate and kidded her about being a visionary.

She replied that he had a great deal to learn about himself and every human being had the same ability if they would only take the time and put in the effort to develop it. As their conversation had become more intense she had told him to always be aware of strangers passing through his life, for they had often come to deliver a message and then be gone. Peggy had felt these should be regarded as messages from God to help us on our life journey and that it was our job to pay attention to them. The conversation had recurred to him again and again over the ensuing years.

He recalled they had been sitting at the table in the courtyard of the pension and she had laughingly looked through the open door into his room and asked, "Have you read all of those books in there?" He had replied, "No, but at the right time I probably will." She had turned to him and with the serious expression of one about to share a rule of life had responded, "That is exactly what I am talking about. Books serve us just as people do. A book will come to you when you need it. Always be receptive to reading books that your intuition guides you to."

At the time he had thought she was putting far too much importance onto what were simply chance encounters of an active life. Periodically over the years as he recalled their conversation he had given thought to her statements but had always felt that he was a realist and was far too logical to allow that type of thinking to guide his life. He had lain the book THINK AND GROW RICH by his bedside fully intending to read it. Interestingly he had not yet ever read the book.

He and Peggy had become good friends during their first year in Guatemala and since they both were far from home for the first time the friendship had become very valuable to them both. Not one time in their two year tour as Volunteers had there been even a hint of romantic interest.

Periodically the Peace Corps would call them all together for a brief training and R&R session and in 1964 one of those sessions had taken place at Lake Atitlan.

Lake Atitlan was a beautiful site high in the mountains bordered by volcanoes with ancient Indian villages around the edges of the lake. Not many miles away were Spanish churches dating back to the 1600's. One Saturday afternoon all twenty-seven of the Volunteers had been pulled together for a Navy doctor from the U.S. Embassy to take blood samples and in general give them all physicals and determine if they were still healthy.

The day turned into a particularly beautiful evening and Peggy and Luke had wound up sitting on some rocks warm from the sun at the waters edge. They had watched several Indians paddle slowly by and as the sun set over one of the volcanoes the moon had risen in all of its Mayan splendor and was reflecting off the water.

That evening as they sat in the warmth left behind by the falling sun they had talked about their families, their homes and the hundred other things that two people far from home for the first time and missing all they had left behind will often share. As Luke and Peggy sat there by Lake Atitlan they had been joined by five or six other Volunteers and for several hours they shared the experiences they were each having in their own separate villages. As they began to break up for the night they had all agreed they should visit each other in their own villages so they could all see as much of Guatemala as possible. Because of this, during Luke's time in Guatemala, he was able to travel over the entire country.

That night, before they parted to their separate rooms for the night Peggy had said to Luke, "Remember what I said, Luke, about people coming into our lives for a purpose. The conversations we had tonight there by the Lake with the other Volunteers are important to how we use the rest of our time here in Guatemala."

Luke had decided as he sat listening to the river with his morning coffee that he needed to go back to the Meier and Frank store at noon and stand under the clock. Just perhaps, the escalator woman might work there and come down the escalator on her way to lunch. Each day that week he had done exactly the same thing. Dressing each morning with the greatest care he arranged his schedule so he was able to be under the clock by about eleven-thirty and he drifted around the area looking at shirts, women's handbags, and perfume. As he moved around the store he always kept a close watch on the escalator. By the third day he was beginning to chide himself about his senseless quest but something deep inside him kept him coming back. He did not behave this way normally and even though it bothered him he continued and each day he had returned to take up his vigil to find her.

On Friday, as the noontime crowd began to lessen, he looked up from a shirt he had been holding and realized a clerk was standing behind the counter directly in front of him. She seemed years past retirement age but said in a clear strong voice, "May I help you, sir?"

"No thanks, I'm just looking."

"Yes, I know. I have seen you here all week long. May I ask what you are searching for?"

He looked at her carefully and thought, "Well, why not?" "Perhaps you could help me. Last week I was standing here beneath the clock waiting for my brother and there was a woman came down the escalator. She had coal black hair, green eyes, the most beautiful smile, is about 5'5" and has a very nice figure. Does that mean anything to you?"

A quizzical smile played across her face as she replied, "Perhaps, that could be Miss O'Connor. She is Director of Human Relations and works on the Fifth Floor. But, I believe she is on vacation for two weeks. Is she the reason you have been loitering around here everyday for the past week?"

"Was I that obvious?"

"Yes, you were. All dressed up with no where to go, I wondered what you might be up to."

"You said she is off for two weeks, that means she has another week to go, right?"

"Tell me why you have been waiting around here each day."

"Actually, I am a little unclear about that myself. I was absolutely stricken by her looks and when we saw each other for just a moment she smiled and I thought...."

"Yes, you thought, "What a beautiful young woman, I need to get to know her."

Unaccustomed to such directness from a woman old enough to be his grandmother, Luke had quietly responded, "Yes, that's right, I feel compelled to meet her."

"When we listen to our intuitive instincts that is often what it is like young man. What is your name?"

"Luke."

"That sounds Biblical. Is it?"

"Well, I grew up in a small country Church and my brother's name is Mark, so you are probably right."

"Would you like to meet our Kathryn, Luke?"

"Of course, that is why I have been coming here." Luke briefly told her about himself and a little of his background, he knew from the way she nodded her head she believed him.

Suddenly she interrupted him, "My, I have to get back to work here. Luke, you be right here by my counter next Tuesday at 11:45. You will not regret being here!"

The entire next week Luke had been on the proverbial pins and needles waiting in eager anticipation. Finally! Tuesday! As he showered and shaved he thought of what he should wear. Casual? Business suit? Should he invite her to lunch? Finally he picked a light brown suit, an off-white French cuff shirt and a blue and brown patterned tie. Just last week a woman at church had complimented him on the same outfit and he was confident it looked sharp.

Parking his car in a nearby lot he entered the store and saw his new friend standing behind her counter. She smiled knowingly as she saw him and motioned him over in front of her.

"She should be down in just a moment, Luke. It is her regular routine. My, you look handsome this morning. You should be working in our men's department over there, we have a difficult time finding men who know how to dress well and coordinate their clothing."

They continued to talk for a few moments until he saw her look past him and say, "Kathryn, this is the gentleman I mentioned to you. This is Luke."

As he turned a series of things happened all at once. It registered in his mind that she had said, "The gentleman I mentioned to you." By then he had turned and the onslaught on his mind continued. She was absolutely beautiful! That long black hair shone in the store lights and curled around her face in a perfect frame as it dropped onto the slope of her shoulders. Those incredible eyes were exactly as he remembered them and up close they were even more luminescent than his memory of them.

What was she saying? Something about she must be going or she would miss lunch. It certainly had been nice to meet him. He had asked her to allow him to take her to lunch and in one short hour they had come to know each other in ways he never thought possible. They talked about her job and her family. She shared with him the story of how she had grown up in Ridgewood, New Jersey and had been transferred out to Portland a few years before by an employment agency she had worked for at the time. Kathryn had loved growing up in Ridgewood, especially at Christmas time when they lit up a huge evergreen tree at one end of the main street. Kathryn excitedly told him about the main street with its numerous small shops and cafes. There was always something happening in the Village, as she referred to it, and she had been especially conscious growing up of the many cultural activities that took place. Kathryn was very proud of The Ridgewood Concert Band, directed she said by Dr. Chris Wilhjelm, which had traveled all over the world to play some of the finest concert music. She laughed and had told him that even though she now lived nearly three thousand miles away she still purchased a season ticket to their concerts. Her eyes had glowed and sparkled as she told him how they played Holiday music in the park during the lighting of the Christmas tree. Kathryn had continued telling him about the beautiful park in the very center of town where she would often take her lunch and watch the people walking to and fro on their way about their business. The tall trees in the block square park cast shade on hot summer days that gave a wonderful respite for a few moments. The soldiers memorial on one side of the central grassy area held the inscribed names of the sons of many families that had lived in the Village for generations. She had enthusiastically told him how her father for nearly twenty years had sung bass with the Orpheus Club Men's Chorus, conducted by John Palatucci. The Orpheus Club had for years been recognized as one of the oldest and most well organized men's singing clubs in the northeast. Each year she looked forward with eager anticipation to their annual Spring Concert. He could tell how much she loved her hometown and how much she missed it.

They talked about his consulting business, the work he was doing with The War on Poverty and his time in Guatemala with the Peace Corps. He explained that he had never really discovered exactly what he wanted to do for a career except that in the past he had wanted to follow in his father's footsteps in the timber industry. How or, even more importantly, to what extent he wanted to devote his life to timber he had never really determined. His time with the Peace Corps and the War on Poverty had shown him very clearly that at some point he wanted to work with projects which would benefit people in a way that was more than just an employment opportunity. His most serious thought had been he would go to work for a major company and hopefully work his way over the years into upper management. He had realized in his Senior year in Forestry at Oregon State that the small to middle level timber companies needed help in managing their timber cuts but they were limited in how many people they could directly employ to provide that management service for themselves. A few months before he actually graduated, one of his professors had come to him with the man who would eventually become his first client. The professor had suggested Luke work with him a few hours each week as a consultant.

Sitting there telling Kathryn about how he was trying to determine how deeply he wanted to become committed to the timber industry Luke never would have anticipated that a little over twenty years later he would be faced with many of those same questions and decisions again.

CHAPTER FOUR

"Until you select a definite purpose in life you
dissipate your energies and spread your thoughts
over so many subjects and in so many different directions
that you lead not to power but to indecision and weakness."

Napoleon Hill

Once again Luke realized his pipe had gone out. Kathryn had apparently come out onto the porch because there beside him was a glass of his favorite homemade lemonade. He watched the river sliding by below thinking of how he had taught each of their children, including the girls, how to fish down there in the eddy that formed where the river made a slight bend. How very fortunate he and Kathryn had been the last few years! As he sat in the warm shade of the porch his thoughts moved back to the events of the past that had made definite changes in his life.....

Luke stared down at his coffee cup. Man alive! What had happened?! How could he be without a job? The past week had become a blur, with each day blending into the next and each meeting or conversation becoming a part of the previous one. He had always been a leader, the one in the group that was often the decision maker. In grade school in gym class he was always one of the captains who got to choose from the other kids to create one of the teams. In high school he had been a class officer, football team captain, on the honor roll and always had a girlfriend. In college and even later in the Peace Corps people had deferred to him for guidance. This couldn't be happening to him! This sort of thing happened to "other people."

Now suddenly, after nearly twenty years of having helped Tom Simon to guide Mt. Hood Land and Cattle Co. through arguments over water rights, land zoning and the fluctuations of the timber market he was regarded as expendable by the new owners of Mt. Hood Land and Cattle. When Tom, sole owner of Mt. Hood Land and Cattle, had died suddenly early this year Luke had fully expected that Tom's heirs would keep the company going just as the preceeding owners had in their family for generations. The company had actually existed for over a hundred and twenty years. But, much to his surprise and to the astonishment of the local business community, Tom's family had quietly made outside contacts and then as a purchase was nearing completion had moved quickly to complete the deal.

More than three hundred people, from tree fallers to log truck drivers and a few executives like himself who had spent most of their lives learning how to survive in the timber industry were swiftly told the doors were closing. The new owners felt the timber industry in the Northwestern part of the United States was never going to regain its former economic power and they were moving on to greener pastures.

Luke should have seen this change coming but had kept his own hopes alive that he would be able to continue his comfortable income by becoming a timber broker. Now he realized there would always be some brokers who dealt with specialty lumber but the days of trainload sales of lumber were gone forever. The entire world was changing and sitting here this morning Luke realized for the first time, like it or not, he was being forced to change with it. That was one thing he definitely had learned through his two years as a Peace Corps Volunteer. Always be prepared to be flexible. The Northwest he had grown up in had certainly changed. For one thing the population had exploded with people moving into the Northwest from all over the country, and even other parts of the world, to be able to have a more "natural" lifestyle. There was developing in Northwest society a personal attitude on the part of many newcomers that was greedier for personal gain than when he had been a boy. Yes, it had been a totally different world then and as the culture of the nation began to change he had felt he had kept abreast of those changes by opening his own life to acceptance of new cultures and the people he worked with who had different ancestral heritages than his own. He had always been thankful for the two years in Guatemala where the culture had been so vastly different than the one he had known in Oregon.

His coffee had grown cold that morning without his realizing it. As he raised the cup to his lips it tasted as though it had been in front of him for hours rather than the last twenty minutes. The paper he had been looking through listed lots of different jobs; none of which seemed to fit his background nor did he feel he could qualify for many of them. Strange how the job market was so very different than it had been just a few years ago when he had graduated from Oregon State University with his degree in Forestry Management. Back then the timber companies had come to the university campuses actually looking for fresh young graduates to fill the many jobs in what was looked upon as the base industry of the Northwest economy. He had been in demand then! For the first time in his life he was realizing that not only did nobody want him, but they really didn't need him! How could an entire lifestyle and society have apparently left him behind and he hadn't even realized it? Just a few months ago he recalled having read a newspaper article about one of the major auto makers in the Midwest laying off over 20,000 people. He had felt sorry for them but had actually felt somewhat removed from their personal plight. This morning sitting here with his cup of coffee he realized exactly what they must have felt like when the solid company they had worked for all of their lives told them that in three weeks they would no longer be needed. "And oh, in addition we have discovered our pension program has been overextended and the retirement resources you thought you developed are not going to be there for you."

Over the past year he had read in the Oregonian Newspaper about thousands of other people being laid off across the country by the large industrial giants, not only the automobile industry, and the news articles talked about "job training," "new industry counseling" and other terms that basically were nice ways of telling experienced hard working people that if they wanted a job they needed to develop new skills. Why, just the other day he had even read an article in Fortune Magazine that said a large number of skilled executives just like himself never truly were able to return to the same type of work they had been forced to leave. If they did they often had to take a substantial pay cut.

The little waitress with the short blonde hair and the sharp eyes looked at him as she walked past the counter. This was the third day in a row he had come in and seated himself at the counter. He felt as though he had a sign across his forehead that read, "Out of Work." He had never felt this way in his entire life and frankly he had no idea what he was going to do. Each morning he had come in, asked for coffee with cream, and opened the paper to read the want ads. Each morning as his coffee grew cold he had read through the ads for nurses, sales reps, hair dressers, veterinary assistants, and all kinds of other advertisements that had absolutely nothing to offer him. He was realizing this morning this was not the way for him to go. He needed to do something else. But what? He had heard of a special counselor who apparently was having success in helping people find employment but the question really was, "WHAT DO I DO NOW?"

As he sipped cold coffee the young blonde appeared again and he let her empty his cup before she filled it with steamy hot brew made with beans from a local coffee roaster. He had started to come to this cafe three days ago because he could not stand to sit at their kitchen table at home and have Kathryn continually looking at him as though saying, "Why haven't you found a job and gotten yourself started over?" The first six weeks she had been understanding. He had gone for nine interviews in that time and each time had been told, "Luke, you are just way too qualified for the position we have available. We'll keep your resume in our file."

Or the job had been so menial that he would have been embarrassed to death to even tell his neighbors what he was doing. Then, the "looks" from Kathryn had started. So, on Monday morning he had showered put on a suit and tie and left the house. This coffee shop had seemed a convenient place to try to get himself organized. But, nothing was happening! He was young enough to take a few classes at the local Community College to acquire some new skills but what should they be?

At first it had been a shock to realize he had joined the ranks of thousands across America who had been downsized or their employment ended for some obscure reason. The man at the little table to the left of the cafe entrance had a paper and a cup of coffee just as he did. They had looked at each other several times the past three days. Once Luke had the fleeting thought that he and the man across the coffee shop should start their own club and call it the "Unemployed Entrepreneurs Club."

Luke had read recently in a popular news magazine that all across America the thousands of little coffee shops that had sprung up were fast becoming "centers" for this huge club of primarily middle-aged people who were gong in each day, ordering a cup of coffee and then attempting to look busy. With no communication between themselves they had become, through no real fault of their own, a huge pool of educated and trained people that were embarrassed and ashamed to say they were unemployed and, even worse, they were unemployable. Luke knew that was definitely how he felt this morning.

One of the senior members of the church he and Kathryn had attended for the last six or seven years had asked him to come tomorrow morning to a Men's Group Meeting. He had told him there would be people at the meeting he might not know and he would introduce him. Well, at least it was an attempt to enlarge his contact base. He had to give everything a try at this point!

Throughout the day he tried to talk with old friends and business associates from over the years. He even called two old high school buddies that he had played football with, all with no positive results. The responses were always the same, "You'll do fine. I wish there was a way that I could help you, but I don't know of anything right now."

Was it his age? He wasn't that old, yet! It sure wasn't like he was at retirement age or he had been fired for not doing a good job. He had made Tom Simon and Mt. Hood Land and Cattle, Co. a lot of money over the years. Only last year he had been Chairman of the Finance Committee for the Chamber of Commerce and they had raised the $650,000 budget in less time than ever before. People at the bank or their church all recognized him when he walked into a room or a meeting. Luke had always kept himself trim and he had taken pride in always having clothes that were well pressed and coordinated. People had always seemed to respect that he did not enter into a great deal of idle conversation but when he did voice an opinion it was usually worthwhile. All day those same people had been cordial but distant as he explained what had happened at Mt. Hood Land and Cattle. They had been sympathetic but of absolutely NO HELP in his search for employment.

Was there something he had done that had created this situation? He had gone to college and followed a fairly common pathway into developing a "career." His major difference had been the two years he was in Guatemala. Those two years had broadened him so much and he always remembered them with pride. But here, several decades later they were certainly not helping him to find a job! He had contacted the Peace Corps office in Washington, D.C. and been told they would contact him if they had anything to talk about. No call had come. Everyone had always said that most people didn't really ever follow a career path they had trained for in college so he had felt pretty good about how his career had developed with Mt. Hood Land and Cattle. Where had his life changed in such a way that he had become so unqualified for any type of meaningful employment? His political contacts had even been unable to provide any hope for job contacts or connections.

His father had worked in the woods as a tree faller all his life and on the side he had a small acreage where they had raised strawberries for some extra income. Luke's life as a teenager had been fairly ordinary. His mother and father had required that the whole family attend church every Sunday and even though it bored him as he got older he had continued to attend out of respect for his parents. Life had been fun and for the most part enjoyable. He did remember that as he grew through his teenage years there had been times when he wondered where life would take him and what it would take for him to learn what life was really all about.

As a teenager one of his challenges at church had been the entire concept of what wealth was and what it really meant to be wealthy. He knew even today it always bothered him that he and Kathryn were able to "live better" with his position at Mr. Hood Land and Cattle than many of the people in their community. There had been a dichotomy during his youth he had never been able to fully understand and by the time he was entering his twenties he had put it into the back of his mind where it didn't really bother him. The conflict had been fairly simple; If wealth and money really were evil then why were the church leaders and the respected members of society all "well off" financially?

It did not occur every Sunday but it happened often enough that by the time he was ten or eleven it was an accepted part of his religious background. "Wealth was evil!!" How many times had he heard it quoted from the pulpit of their small country church, "It is easier for a camel to pass through the eye of a needle, than for a rich man to enter into the Kingdom of God."

It had always troubled him that as he sat in church and listened to those many sermons he used to look around him and the church Elders and Trustees were always local businessmen who were very successful financially. He remembered more than once watching the man who owned the major hardware store in town, who obviously made a great deal of money, sit in his pew nodding his head in agreement as a pastor quoted James 5:1 and 2, "Go to now, ye rich men, weep and howl for your miseries that shall come upon you. Your riches are corrupted, and your garments are moth eaten."

He had always struggled with why the employer in the Gospel of Mathew in The Bible took the talent from the man who had buried it and gave it to the one who doubled his talents through trading. Somehow that story had never fit with the ones about riches being evil.

He remembered as he was growing up hearing someone refer to the Language of Money. There had been a series of phrases about money that were supposedly pieces of wisdom about its use. They had included, "You can't take it with you," "Save for a Rainy Day," "The more money you have, the more you need," "All money does is create problems," and then the misquote he had heard all his life, "Money is the root of all evil." He had been in his twenties before he had realized the actual quote is, "The <u>love</u> of money is the root of all evil." He knew at that point there was a big difference between the real quote and the misquote but he still had struggled with the concept of money and its use.

There was one thing he did know however and for this reason he had always had a job in high school. The best looking girls in school always wanted to go out with the boys who had a car and money in their pockets to spend! Once he had learned that rule of life he had always worked hard to have money in his pocket.

Often as he became a young adult and especially as he graduated from college and began to plan his adult life, those early teachings would come back to him as he pondered where he wanted his life to go. One thing he had come to realize in Guatemala very clearly, being poor was not where he wanted to be in life! Almost everyone in Tierra Fuerte had been at a subsistence level income and he had learned early in those two years there was nothing pious about being poor.

His foot accidentally hit his worn leather briefcase sitting by his feet here in the little coffee shop. How many years ago had Tom given him the beautiful old case? As he looked at it laying by his foot he suddenly realized all four of the corners that sat on the floor were worn and frayed. The sides were marked and scarred after years of having been tossed into the back of a pick-up truck or propped up on a stump on the side of a hill being logged off. There was even a deep scratch on one side where years ago a careless yardboy at one of their mills had allowed a razor sharp axe he had been carrying to slice the beautiful leather. Something about the old leather case continued to nag at him as he stuffed his newspaper into it and got up to leave. Was it that the old bag somehow represented where he was in life and he did not recognize the need to change both his old worn briefcase and his life direction?

At home that evening Kathryn was quiet as she prepared dinner and he did not know what to say to her. She was obviously losing patience with him. Didn't she understand he was doing everything possible to find a job! Didn't she read the papers? Didn't she realize that what was happening to him was happening to thousands of others just like himself all across the country? The circumstances varied from area to area, in some places it was timber, in some the aircraft industry, in others it was the Internet. Who cared anyway what the reasons were---they were all out of work with no place to go! The placement programs really didn't seem to be of much help. Yesterday he had talked with a man about being "retrained" to work in the computer field. He had no interest in computers, he had always hated school and most of all he sure didn't want to spend the next ten to twenty years chained to a desk in somebody else's office!

He had thought briefly about writing, but that was almost scarier than having been ousted from his job. He had no way of assuring himself anything he wrote would ever sell! Momentarily he had thought about selling the beach house but he knew that would break Kathryn's heart. The whole family loved that retreat! What was really killing him was the way Kathryn had started going through their home and was taking item after item down to a secondhand shop where she was selling some of her prized possessions for a mere pittance in order not to take the last drop of their savings to maintain their home. She had not said a word to him but he knew that she had taken her grandmother's silver tea service down and sold it.

Years before while living in Guatemala he remembered he had stopped his Jeep beside a beautiful open space in the jungle several kilometers outside Tierra Fuerte. He had intended to sit quietly for a few moments and smoke his pipe. He soon realized that from a nearby tree at least three pairs of dark black eyes were watching him as well. He had only seen monkeys once before in the weeks he had been in Tierra Fuerte. As he watched all three of

51

the small nimble animals began to move from tree to tree deeper into the jungle. Leaving his pipe in the Jeep he had begun to follow them.

Twenty minutes later he stopped. Where was he? The jungle had seemed to close in around him and he had been so intent on following the monkeys he had totally lost track of where he had gone! For a moment he felt a surge of adrenalin and panic. No one knew he was out here! He had no compass!

Having grown up in the forests of Oregon he knew that the first thing he needed to do was stop. Be quiet. Then determine where he had come from so that he could retrace his steps and return to his Jeep. Thirty minutes later he emerged out of the jungle only about twenty yards up the road from his Jeep. Smiling to himself in relief he realized the jungle could be even more deceptive than the forests of the Northwest.

Sitting here this evening he felt much as he had for the few minutes when he had lost his way in the dense Guatemalan jungle. He knew he must very soon be producing some income. But he could not seem to find a way that would lead him out of this dense maze he was in.

The alarm jerked him awake the next morning with just enough time to shower, shave and get to the church for the Men's Group Meeting. As he rolled out of his side of the king size bed he and Kathryn had shared for over three decades he marveled again at how fortunate he had been to be standing at the bottom of that escalator years before. That was definitely one area of his life that had gone extremely well. Even though they had been short with each other recently and had small arguments over money he knew she loved him and that they always belonged together. A dog barking somewhere outside jerked him back into the present. He looked at the warm bed he had just left. All of their married life Kathryn had never lost her ability to excite him and enchant him with her very personal sensuality. Last night she had chosen to wear a loose flowing black satin nightgown that this morning was bunched up around her thighs leaving her legs exposed to his loving eyes. Maybe he could just lay back down with her for a few minutes and they could hold each other close. That would feel so good and as always they could comfort each other.

No! He must get started quickly. This morning he had an appointment that perhaps could be very meaningful for him and his family, even though frankly right now he could not see how it might become important. Putting on a pair of dark blue slacks and a blue-brown patterned sport coat over a light blue button down shirt with a dark blue tie and a red design he felt ready to go see what might happen. He had always enjoyed dressing well. Knowing he was well dressed always gave him a feeling of confidence and this morning was no exception. Who do you suppose might be at this meeting he had been invited to attend?

CHAPTER FIVE

"My rich dad said, 'The richest people
in the world look for and build networks,
everyone else is trained to look for work.'"

Robert E. Kiyosaki

Letting himself in the side door of the great stone church building he had come to enjoy so much he realized the building was still chilly from the cool spring night and there was no one else around. A sign on the office window told him the 6:30 AM Men's Bible Study was downstairs in the kitchen annex. Did he smell hot coffee? That would taste good right now. Eight or nine men in various types of dress sat around the large table that the church staff used during the day for coffee, lunch, and other types of activities. It had a certain homey atmosphere that it gave to the small group. His friend Bobby---everyone called him "Bobby" even though he was well into his seventies..... stood up as he came into the room and greeted him warmly. Several of the other men he had met in church said hello. One thing that he had learned about a church with two thousand members, you really only got to know a few of the people, certainly not the entire congregation. The others introduced themselves as he shook hands around the table. Someone handed him a cup of hot steamy coffee in a church mug apparently left over from some long ago fund raiser. The mug felt warm and comfortable in his hands. Safe. Funny how that word popped into his mind. The group obviously, though small, had been meeting together for a number of years. The next hour went swiftly as they read from the Bible and discussed the verses they had read. At the end of their time the leader looked at Bobby with a question in his eyes and Bobby immediately said, "I know you all had the opportunity to meet our new friend Luke but I have asked him here this morning for a very specific reason. Luke, this is not a support group, even though sometimes we act like one. We are a Bible Study Group and upon occasion we help each other with things that may even be totally unrelated to the church activities. This group started over twenty years ago and several of us have been in the group from its first meeting. As you have probably noticed we do not have a pastor here this morning and the leader of the group rotates on a monthly basis so that it is one of us leading to the best of our ability. The value of this group has been that we can talk about anything and sometimes our conversations go a long way from just the Scripture that we happen to be reading on any particular morning. We have experienced the deaths of friends and spouses, community problems and as you are experiencing right now, the need perhaps for some lifestyle changes." Turning back to the group Bobby said, "Luke has a personal challenge which has come about because of all the changes at Mt. Hood Land and Cattle over the past few months and I asked him to come and share his story with us to see if any of us might be of help to him. Luke, take a few minutes and tell us what is happening in your life right now."

Fortunately Luke had always been comfortable speaking with groups and the next five minutes went quickly as Luke explained his background and gave a somewhat vague idea of what he was looking for. They all showed the proper sympathy, a few words were offered of support and in the final prayer the leader asked for God's help in finding a solution to Luke's challenge.

As everyone was filing out a man dressed much as he was in a sport coat and slacks reached out his hand and said, "Luke, I'm Dave. Do you have time for a cup of coffee?" The thought ran through Luke's head that he really had nothing else to do but he had better be careful not to have to spend too much money. He heard himself responding, "Sure, what did you have in mind?"

The man ignored his question as they continued out onto the street but rather began to ask him questions about Mt. Hood Land and Cattle, his family and what he had done over the years. He seemed particularly interested in Luke's time in the Peace Corps and what it had meant to him. The questions allowed them to enter into an easy conversation that carried them down the street to a nearby Starbuck's. As they ordered coffee Dave quickly paid and they moved to a corner table.

"How long can you take, Luke? I have about forty-five minutes before my first appointment." Luke stated in a vague way he could take whatever time he needed but he had something to do later in the morning himself. For several minutes the conversation seemed to go nowhere when Dave suddenly said, "Luke, what do you really want to do now that you are free to make the choice to do whatever you want?"

The phrasing of the question took Luke by surprise. "Do whatever you want?" He had not really thought of his plight as offering him the opportunity "to do whatever you want." Did Dave understand he needed a job? Income? Someway to provide for Kathryn and himself and to make his regular car and house payments? What did Dave mean? Was the guy going to turn out to be some kind of kook? Luke countered with a question to Dave, "Why did you want to have coffee? What do you do? Tell me a little about yourself."

Dave responded by sharing with Luke that he had two children, a boy and a girl, he and his wife, Jana, had been married for ten years, his wife was a CPA and he had met her through a consulting job years before. As Dave's story progressed Luke realized he had a fairly substantial income, he and his wife traveled more than most people and Luke also realized he had learned very little about what Dave really did to create his lifestyle. Finally Dave finished by returning to the same question he had asked earlier, "So, Luke, if you were to take a piece of paper and a pen and write one sentence describing what you would like to do with your new found freedom, what would it say?"

This guy wouldn't let up! Where was his logic coming from? And yet Luke felt that what Dave was saying to him was the same question he had been asking himself the last few days, "WHAT DO I DO NOW?" Obviously he could write down he wanted to find a job paying him enough to continue living the way he and Kathryn had become accustomed to for the last several years. But, he knew this was not the kind of answer Dave was looking for. Just out of college he had wanted to start his own timber company. He had put that off until he came back from the Peace Corps. He had started his own little consulting business instead. He had worked simultaneously at his position with The Office of Economic Opportunity and had consequently developed a much broader background than many people his same age. It was through his consulting work that he had then met Tom Simon and been offered the job with Mt. Hood Land and Cattle. That first job had been an executive position with responsibility for governmental affairs and relations and then eventually he had become Tom's right-hand man. He knew the company inside and out and had never really thought much after he was with Tom about what he really wanted to do with his life. He had a good job. It paid well. He enjoyed the work. He was outdoors enough that he didn't feel confined. The twenty years he had been with Mt. Hood Land and Cattle had not really flown by, until he looked back at them, but rather they had drifted past much like a puffy white cloud in the sky that moves according to where the wind takes it. He had become very comfortable with the relationship he had with Tom. Any thought of what he might do after Mt. Hood Land and Cattle just never seemed to be of any great importance. Oh sure, he and Kathryn had talked between themselves about retirement at some vague point in the future and they had several times attempted to start a retirement fund or financial program but there always seemed to be something more important at the moment that would alter whatever savings they were attempting to build. With four children they had always seemed to have someplace to use any extra money they had created. They had always been comfortable and the beach house had been their sanctuary.

Then, boom! Everything had changed! Now, here was Dave asking him a question that frankly he could not answer.

"Dave, maybe that is part of my challenge right now. I have been so surprised by being laid off I don't really know what I want to do next."

Dave accepted his answer with no comment. No smile. No condescending words. No response except to open his briefcase and take out a book which he laid by his coffee cup.

"Luke, I want you to do something for me. I'm going to give you a book. I want you to browse through it. Read the first chapter and read one or two others that catch your attention. I give people this book once in a while to help them work through exactly where you are in your life. This is the book." Dave held up a copy of THINK AND GROW RICH by Napoleon Hill.

"Have you ever read this book before, Luke?"

"No, I haven't but Tom Simon had a copy of it on the shelf behind his desk where he always worked. I even bought a copy of it back when I lived in Guatemala but I never seemed to have enough time to stop and read it."

"You never read it? Too bad. But, that's OK. Here is what I want you to do. Like I said, browse through the book. It is probably too much to read in one day but study it as well as you can. Then I want you to meet me right here tomorrow morning at 8:00 for another cup of coffee and we will talk about the book."

"Dave, that is all well and good, but I need to get a job, not read books!"

Dave laughed as he responded, "I know. Believe me, I understand a lot better than you think I do. Read the book as I said. Let me buy you a cup of coffee in the morning. What have you got to lose? One day! One day that may open your thoughts in ways you have never considered! That book did for me! It has helped tens of thousands of others! Tomorrow, if you read the book, I may be able to help you." Dave had been writing something in the book as he talked and as he stood he left the book face up on the table in front of Luke and put a red felt tip pen beside it. After he walked out the door Luke opened the book and found the following on the inside flap:

Luke,

Upon occasion I meet someone I feel can truly

benefit from reading this book. This could be

one of the most important days in your life. Read

the first chapter with care! Browse through

the rest of the book. Make notes about what you are

thinking as you read. Trust me, this will be time

well spent!

Your friend, Dave

Well, Luke thought it has been quite a long time since anyone gave me a book, so I guess I have nothing to lose. Perhaps I'll start right now. As Luke began to read he realized much of what Napoleon Hill had to say Luke had read in other books over the years. Tom Simon, who Luke was beginning to think he should have used more as a business mentor than he had, had used more than one of the sayings in the book and had set goals for his personal life just as Hill described. Luke did remember the book on Tom's bookshelf had looked particularly worn and was well used. The chapter on how to use a Mastermind was interesting. Tom had used the Executive Committee in just that way. Why had he never read this book before? But then how could a book help him get past where he was at the moment? In fact, he probably should not be wasting his time! This book spent a great deal of time talking about dreams, goals, and things like a life purpose. As Luke thought about what he was reading in the book he realized his new friend, Dave, had asked him the very same questions earlier in the day THINK AND GROW RICH was forcing him to think about right now. What do you suppose would happen if he actually did begin to write down some of the things he wanted to accomplish? He laid his yellow tablet out beside the book and began to jot down thoughts and ideas as they came to him. He would read for awhile, stop and think about what he had read and almost always have some thought that felt as though it needed to be put on his notepad. It had been a long time since he last took time to do this kind of exercise. Without realizing it he already had written down a number of things he wanted to accomplish with the rest of his life. Just the process of doing this had given him an uplifting feeling he could not fully understand. It was as though he had made a very positive move in the right direction and he felt an increased confidence in taking this time to read and to talk with Dave.

People were going in and out of the Starbuck's as Luke continued to read. Finally he stood and getting a coffee to go he began walking down the street to his car. He had always loved Portland in the spring and this morning was a perfect example of why he felt that way. The flowers were bursting out, the grass was a bright green, the sky was a beautiful blue and the total ambiance of the new day and the new life springing forth was exhilarating. Should he stop someplace here in town to read some more? No, he knew what to do. He had always felt that Washington Park in the West Hills above the city was one of the most beautiful public parks anywhere in the world. Many years ago the city had developed, through a civic group called The Portland Rose Society, a rose show and test garden which over the decades had become much more than any of the original founders probably ever imagined. Bordered on the west by huge rhododendron bushes of many hues and colors the Garden now sprawled across the side of the West Hills and overlooked the downtown section of the city.

After World War I and again following World War II special commemorative areas with small secluded nooks and benches had been created and on any semi-warm day there would be people of all ages seated on the benches reading, thinking or simply relaxing. Even on days when there was a mist in the air, romance could be seen developing throughout the Park as couples walked hand-in-hand along the grassy trails between the rosebuds. He would drive up into the Park and find a place in the sun where he could read and think about what Dave had started with his simple gift of a book.

His life had followed a fairly even path as he had worked for Mt. Hood Land and Cattle. He had been the same as the rest of the people that he knew and over the years his family had lived well, they had a nice home, and always drove a new car but his life had not been guided by any type of real purpose, as Napoleon Hill talked about in his book. In high school no teacher or counselor had ever talked with him about what he really wanted to contribute to society or about "fulfilling his dreams." Whenever he had talked with a counselor it had always been about how to get into college or what he wanted to study at the university. He had taken aptitude tests and talked with people on career days but he could not remember any one of his high school teachers ever talking about writing down goals or working on the development of a "life purpose." He really had no idea what his life purpose was or for that matter even how to go about developing a "life purpose statement." He laughed as he looked around at the trees and the green life appearing. His life purpose had always been to make enough money to take care of Kathryn and provide for his family. But, Hill was talking about something more than that. So was Dave. Luke was positive that tomorrow morning one of the things that Dave would ask him was going to have to do with his own personal life goals.

That could be a tough one to answer. As he continued to read Hill's book he began to understand that the names he knew and respected from industry and business had all followed the outline presented in this little book. Why had no one ever talked with him about this type of thing in high school or in college? Why had they not had some type of class that would have made them all think about what they really wanted to do with their lives? In reality, that had been one of the reasons he had joined the Peace Corps. There was no question that being a Volunteer had helped him see the world differently. It was as though the entire purpose of his education had really been to prepare him to go out into the "work world" and find a job. He had certainly heard that from plenty of teachers over the years! Oh, he could remember certain teachers talking about the value of being a musician or an artist but he could not recall anyone ever seriously discussing where he wanted to go with his life. It had always seemed that the idea of career orientation programs had been aimed at how to earn a living and how to be a good employee. Well, he had certainly been that! Mt, Hood Land and Cattle had certainly never had any complaints. At least not until the day the new owners had told them all they were going to be taking the company in a "new" direction and many of them were not going to fit into the new structure. At that point he had suddenly known a fear and a foreboding he had never experienced before. In one day his security for his family, his marriage and his future was gone! Ever since that day his one thought had been, "WHAT DO I DO NOW?"

The morning had flown by and Luke suddenly realized it was past noon. People had begun to come into the Park and were walking in small animated groups or strolling thoughtfully by themselves. What should he do this afternoon? He felt guilty about not having been out this morning talking with someone about a job and yet somehow he also knew deep within himself that what he was doing right now might well be one of the most important steps of his life.

Fortunately he had kept a small amount of money in a savings account for emergencies but it was beginning to run low and would not last too much longer. In fact, last week he had quietly, without Kathryn seeing him, taken his deer hunting rifle that his father had used for years and then given to him, down to a gun shop and sold it. He had received $120 for it and felt miserable all day. He knew though that he had done the right thing and this would give him a few extra dollars to make it through the next two weeks. He decided that rather than go home he would go down the hill to a deli and get a sandwich he could bring back up with him and continue reading. For some reason which was very difficult for him to fully understand he felt good and yes, even uplifted by what he had done this morning. The afternoon sped by as fast as the morning and by late afternoon Luke had several pages of notes and he had used Dave's red pen to underline a number of passages in the book. Now, what was he going to do with all of this? How was this going to help him make any additional income? What should he tell Kathryn? Would she understand what he had done this morning or would she regard it as just some whim that had taken him away from searching for employment?

Wasn't that interesting! He had unthinkingly used terminology for the pattern of finding "employment" really without thinking in terms of how "employment" would fit into a larger term goal or purpose. Inside himself he knew for a certainty that how he had spent the day reading and thinking in regard to longer term goals had been of real long range value to himself and to his family.

Kathryn greeted him warmly as he came in the door and gave him one of those deep long kisses that over the years he had enjoyed so much. Even their dog seemed happy and in good humor as he jumped and chased his tail in greeting. Kathryn leaned back in his arms and said, "Any luck today?" The thought ran through his mind, "Here we go." He hugged her close and said, "No," he had not had any luck so far today. He knew by the way she responded physically that his answer was heard, accepted and not at all appreciated. They were both tense and were becoming short with each other in ways they never had been in the past. The kiss when he came home had been warm and welcoming. Her welcome had cooled but she still showed in little ways she loved and supported him.

Later as they sat at the kitchen table and were quietly discussing the things that had taken place during the day they came to a time in the evening that had over the years become very important to them.

When they had first begun to date, to really know each other and to talk about the many things in life that young couples about to marry discuss, the subject of church attendance, faith and prayer had naturally come into the conversation.

Kathryn had said to Luke one evening, "Luke, did your parents pray other than to say grace at meals or when they were in church?"

Luke's response had been, "I think so. The reason I say it that way is because even though my brother and I obviously grew up in their home they were very private about their personal life together. I always had the understanding that they did pray together when they were alone. Why do you ask?"

Kathryn's answer had set the pattern for the rest of their life together, "My parents prayed together and with the family about all kinds of things. I would like for us to do the same. In fact, I would like to start right now even though we are not married yet because we certainly are a couple and intend to share our lives."

That night had started a practice they seldom had deviated from after becoming a married couple. Each night they stopped and, sitting together, they would spend a few minutes in their own silent prayer and then holding hands they would verbally pray together. This had become a very important ritual of their life as a couple and a family.

Tonight they had followed the same pattern but there had been an obvious strain on both their parts. Luke knew more certainly than ever before that he must make something happen with his income very quickly.

The next morning with the thoughts of the strain of the evening before still lingering with him he showered and as he stood before the mirror to shave he saw a note that Kathryn had put up the day before, "We are moving forward each day because the worst is behind us and the best is yet to come." As he left the house to meet Dave he thought again as he had so many times before what a wonderful woman he had married. He felt a certain amount of unexplained eager anticipation as he parked his car and walked to the Starbuck's. As he entered he saw Dave was already there and was talking quietly to a man at the table next to him.

Luke sat down with his own coffee, which he discovered Dave had already paid for, and Dave greeted him with a smile and a handshake. As Dave turned to Luke to begin their conversation he handed the fellow he had been talking with one of his business cards with the statement, "If I can be of any help give me a call." This morning Dave was dressed more casually than yesterday but even with an open neck button-down shirt, sport coat and slacks he looked like a successful businessman. His shoes were shined with a high gloss that implied how expensive they probably were.

Luke had grown up wearing boots and had lived around loggers who wore calks and other heavy duty footgear everyday but he never had forgotten how his father made him shine his shoes every Saturday night to wear to church on Sunday morning. He remembered a comment Tom Simon had made several years ago in the office one morning. Tom loved to wear low heeled cowboy boots and he had come into the office with a new pair that were polished to a gloss so that it seemed you could see your reflection in them and Luke had commented on how nice they looked. Tom's reply had been interesting. "You know, Luke, one way I judge a man is by his footwear. If his shoes are polished chances are he takes care of his life also, if they are scuffed up you better watch him because that says a lot about how he feels about his own life." Luke had never forgotten that statement.

Dave smiled and said, "Well, what did you think? Did you get a chance to look through the book?"

Luke laughed as he said, "It was funny, I started reading the first chapter and before I realized it I was into the third chapter and then I took all day actually to read almost the entire book! I don't know how I have reached the age I have and have never read that book before. I've seen it but had never picked it up to read it."

Dave's reply was to come back to Luke many times over the next few years, "I understand. One of the things I have learned about life's process is that people and books come into our lives when they are supposed to. Kind of like the old expression, "when the student is ready, the teacher will appear." Tell me what you thought of the book. Did it make sense?"

Luke's reply was, "How do I answer that! There is so much in that book! I felt like I was being exposed to ideas and thoughts I should have learned years ago! One of the things that really struck me was I really have never thought a whole lot about where I was headed with my life. I have a great wife. She is pretty, sexy and smart. We have four children and we have had a pretty good lifestyle up until now. My whole aim in life has been to provide for them. Oh sure, I'm like everybody else, there have been times when I daydream about what "might have been," but not really very often."

"If you have daydreamed at times, what were the dreams about?"

"Oh, kind of like everybody, a bigger house, a beautiful vacation, being recognized for some great accomplishment. One interesting aspect of that is that ever since I got out of the Peace Corps I have wanted to do something much bigger than just make a living, but everyday life always seemed to get in the way."

"Have you ever thought, like the old saying goes, 'What would you do if money were no object?' "

"I have always thought that was silly---money is always an object."

"OK, then let's say, What would you do if you had been left a large estate and you knew your income needs were totally provided for?"

Luke thought for a moment before he responded, "I do know people have to be involved in doing something. Boredom sets in early and people have to keep busy. I do have some interests, but most people don't know this because I never talk about it. I am an orphan child and even though I grew up in a loving family environment where I was made to truly feel like I was a natural born child I have always wanted to somehow provide love and warmth for orphan kids who are not as fortunate as I was while I was growing up. I would like to write music.

Kathryn and I took a painting class several years ago and we always thought it would be fun to do some creative artwork together."

Dave had been making notes as Luke talked and now he looked up saying, "That is great! See, I knew if somehow we got your juices flowing then you would see some possibilities."

"Sure, Dave, but let's get real. How does this help me to get a job?"

"Luke is it really a job you want or are you looking for something more? Why don't we take a few minutes just to share a little about ourselves with each other." For the next two hours Luke and Dave talked about a hundred different kind of things that seemed to Luke to have absolutely nothing to do with finding him a job. Toward the end of the second hour Luke realized the time had once again flown by and he knew very little about Dave! The entire conversation had been about Luke. Dave was a master at asking the right question at the right moment and he kept the conversation focused on Luke---his past, his family background, Kathryn and what she was like, their children, his hobbies and activities. Even though the two hours had gone swiftly, somehow through it all Luke had developed the very real understanding that Dave truly cared about him as a person and he wanted to be of assistance to him in resolving his challenges. Dave had asked him some difficult questions along with gathering information about Luke's background. At one point they had been talking about Luke's goals in life, as he had expected, and Dave had asked him what "success" meant to him. Luke had really had to work at answering that one and while he was responding he found that he had never really tried to define for himself what "success" meant. Dave had kept after that point like a dog with a bone until finally Luke had said, "You know, I think it actually comes down to being able to live out my personal desires and dreams with Kathryn and make a contribution to the society around us."

Dave had sat back, smiled and asked, "Tired? This has been a lot of work hasn't it? Well, having read most of THINK AND GROW RICH plus just having had this conversation don't you think perhaps the quickest way to find a job might be to decide what you truly want to do with the rest of your life and then fix your focus on that and begin to see what develops? Or you might also consider some type of work that would create a strong residual income that would give you, as a side benefit, enough time to do those other things."

Luke rather hesitantly said, "Sure, but Dave if you are talking about some of these franchises like McDonalds or something like that I don't have anywhere near that kind of money! I don't even have $20,000 to start a business! Besides, Kathryn would kill me if I came home with some crazy scheme that would clean out the last few dollars we have put away!"

Laughing Dave opened his notebook and taking another of his red felt tip pens he turned the pad toward Luke and said, "Write down the figure you would like to have to start per month and then two lines below that number put the lowest figure you would even consider working for per month. Then under that put down how long you have been out of work."

Luke put the numbers down and then looked at Dave.

"Luke, if I could show you how to make your lowest income figure by three months from now and your largest in twelve months would you be interested in talking further?"

Luke nodded his head slowly. He felt he needed to be very cautious right now.

Dave was saying, "What I do Luke is help people start their own businesses. This is nothing new, but some of our ideas are new."

"What do you market? I noticed yesterday that you took some kind of vitamins or something. Does it have anything to do with that?"

"Actually, yes, it does. We market a couple of very unique products that strengthen people's immune systems. We do this through what is called Wellness Marketing which for us has become what is now called a Social Entrepreneur process. It is referred to this way because our company has a sincere interest in helping folks in less fortunate areas of the world to improve their lives and for each supplement product we sell they donate a similar product to projects to help eradicate malnutrition. That part of it is both easy to understand and rather complex scientifically. The other part of what our group does is literally help average people just like you and me to achieve a better place in life and to reach a level of financial security that most of them have never experienced previously. To accomplish this we follow a plan which we call THE FORTUNE FORMULA."

"Do you sell this stuff in stores?"

"No. We have found over the years that working directly one-on-one with individuals like yourself is by far the best way to tell our story. It is also the best way for me to be able to help you, or anyone else, get started in business with me. Have you ever seriously thought about owning your own business, Luke?"

Luke remembered back to years before and how excited he had been when as a recently Returned Peace Corps Volunteer he had started his own consulting business. How much energy he had put into that little business only to have it turn turtle on him at a time when he had really needed the income. The people he had met through his consulting business and his time with the War on Poverty programs had brought him to a new awareness of the importance of politics and who you know in everyday life and that had in turn helped him immensely in his work at Mt. Hood Land and Cattle. Of course, if he had not had the consulting business he never would have been qualified to go to work for Tom Simon anyway. Tom's business had in essence become his own business, but obviously with what had taken place no one in Tom Simon's family had felt the same way at all.

Dave continued, "The plan that I mentioned, THE FORTUNE FORMULA, teaches people how to market small amounts of our products to begin with and then develop business builders like yourself as you grow in the business. A lot of our people refer to going out and finding a job as Plan A. THE FORTUNE FORMULA becomes Plan B or the plan people follow when they can't find a job and have to make changes such as you are experiencing right now. If you work the plan that we have created it will work for you and you can develop an immediate cash income of $2,000 to $3,000 in your third or fourth month. You aren't going to get rich with that but if you continue to follow the plan and do exactly as I teach you it will create $75,000 to $100,000 per year by the end of the third year."

"You would be my teacher?"

"Yes, as closely as possible. As your mentor, part of what I do is "hold your feet to the fire." Dave chuckled and acted almost as if he enjoyed being difficult for those with whom he worked.

"Is this one of those pyramid deals that I have heard about? Kathryn got involved with something called American Style a few years ago and I told her I never wanted to see anything like that in our house again!"

"No. This is not a pyramid. Pyramids are illegal in all fifty states. We have a legitimate system for distributing products directly to the consumer through our Wellness Marketing program. We do not recommend you start by talking with all your neighbors and friends or relatives---in fact, we tell you up front they will probably be the most difficult for you to work with and they will usually be the first to tell you this won't work. No, rather than that type of thing we have a proven program that appeals primarily to two groups of people but actually has applications across the board with both genders and all age groups. The two groups we look to most are people about 18 or 19 up to about 30 who are really struggling to make something happen for themselves and people like yourself who have been downsized, laid off, or "retired" and have a lot to offer as good solid business people. In either case the number one criteria is the same." Dave paused, looking at Luke.

"What is that?"

"We are looking for people who are willing to work hard for a period of time with relatively low income and who understand the principle of delayed gratification and what it means for their family."

"You know, Dave, it is interesting that you refer as you do to delayed gratification. In the timber industry there was a term a few years ago that was "delayed yield" meaning the longer you could put off the harvest of mature trees that still had potential growth the more dollar yield per acre would be achieved."

"You're right! The concept is similar. Now, tell me, how many years were you talking about?"

"With the trees we were working with we were talking 45 to 75 years, often meaning the harvest would occur years, or even decades, after the people responsible for the plantings had passed on."

Dave chuckled, "Man, at least we talk about delayed gratification meaning as taking place during our own working period and being confident we will receive the rewards of our labor ourselves!"

Luke and Dave talked for another half hour before Dave said, "Luke, I have another appointment I have to get to. I want you to take this material and look through it. Who you talk to about this opportunity is totally up to you but I would strongly urge that you not talk to anybody except your wife until you and I talk again. Now I want you to tell me what to do next. You have two options. First option, meet me right here tomorrow at this same time; second option, call me by tomorrow night to set up a time to talk again. I must tell you that if you don't call me by tomorrow night I will not be calling you. As far as I am concerned if you don't call me I will know you are not interested. Which do you want? Meet me here tomorrow or give me a call?"

Something inside Luke was saying very loudly he should meet Dave tomorrow and not delay additional discussions. "Tomorrow, and I will have read through your materials."

"Good, I will tell you right now that at least 75% of the people who tell me they will call me never do! This has become one of my own little ways of separating the chaff from the really good kernels of grain. Another way to say it could be that I use this method to determine who the really serious people are and if they really want to put forth the effort to develop financial security."

Luke's mind was racing as he left the coffee shop. He felt excited, anxious and a fear of the unknown. All at the same time. What was Kathryn's response going to be when he got home?

CHAPTER SIX

"People often ask me how I became successful in that
six year period of time while many of the people I knew
did not. The answer is simple: The things I found easy to do,
they found easy not to do. I found it easy to set the goals that
could change my life. They found it easy not to. I found it easy
to attend the classes and the seminars, and to get around
other successful people. They said it probably wouldn't matter.
If I had to sum it up, I would say what I found to be easy to do,
they found easy not to do. Six years later I'm a millionaire and
they are all still blaming the economy, the government, and
company policies, yet they neglected to do the basic, easy things.

Jim Rohn

It was already afternoon when Luke looked at the little
brown booklet in his hand, EXCERPTS FROM THE
TREASURY OF QUOTES, by Jim Rohn. On the inside there was
a page titled "Dedication" and then on the line titled "To" Dave
had written,

"My new friend Luke"

"Your friend at a point of need"

Dave

What was with this guy anyway? Two meetings in two days and each time a book designed to enhance your life and raise your spirits. Each morning Dave had also paid for the coffee. We'll see what happens tomorrow. Or was this just a part of some "come on" that he hadn't quite caught onto yet? Dave had talked quite a bit about money. No, correct that. Luke could not remember Dave having actually used the word "money" at all. He had spoken of Wealth and Abundance. Money appeared to be something different to Dave than it had always been to Luke.

Luke had grown up with a solid religious background and it was only in the last few years that he had really questioned any of those original teachings. He had never questioned the fundamentals of that faith and his relationship to God but there had been other things he questioned. What about the Creation story he had learned? What role did science play with that story as he had learned it in Sunday School? How had the earth been formed? There were other points he had thought a lot about the last few years but one that for some reason had come to the front of his mind in talking with Dave had been the whole question about money.

How much was enough? How much was too much? What did Dave really mean when he talked about "Abundance" and secure long term income? You worked for your income and if you produced good work you were paid a good salary. Dave had talked about long term gain from work you did early in developing a business. If you collected income for a long length of time after you had completed the actual work how did that really work? Why was he even thinking about this right now anyway? What he really needed to do more than anything else was to begin producing income that could be used to pay his impending bills. They were down to where there was not a whole lot left to draw upon as a reserve. Would he have to sell the beach house or remortgage his home? Even worse, could he even get a mortgage right now with no job? That thought had not even occurred to him before!

If Kathryn realized how close they were to getting to the bottom of the barrel she would not be nearly as understanding.

One thing they had always had between them was a strong physical bond that had created excitement in their lives and brought them joy and contentment. He definitely had to make something happen fast if he was going to keep Kathryn feeling content and secure. He knew that the last couple of weeks she had begun to change. Strange little indications that in one sense were amusing and in another totally different way were extremely disheartening and even alarming. One night about a week ago she had worn a flannel nightgown that she had in the past laughingly referred to as her "granny" gown. His Kathryn, who had always come to their bed in satin and beautiful lace, had definitely been giving him a subliminal message, or at least he thought it was subliminal!

That evening he and Kathryn looked through the little book by Jim Rohn. Kathryn asked, "Have you ever heard of Jim Rohn?"

Luke's response had been that he had seen something about him in magazines over the years but that he really didn't know very much about him except that he apparently did a lot of public speaking for business groups. Luke had never heard him speak and at first was a little curious as to why Dave had even given him the book. As they read pieces to each other the page titles began to make an impression on Luke:

"Personal Development"

"Desire/Motivation"

"Goals/Plans"

Dave had asked Luke questions that had been built around these same points.

Kathryn looked at him with a rather curious expression and said, "Luke, I know you better than anyone else on earth. What would you do right now if you could just do whatever you wanted? You have always talked about traveling and we never have done a whole lot. You used to talk about having your own non-profit charity, remember?"

For the next hour they quietly talked about ideas and dreams they had not talked about together for years. They sat close on the couch in their living room and held hands like teenagers as they restated thoughts and ideas neither of them had mentioned for well over a decade.

Kathryn had always wanted to write and illustrate a children's book but with four children and a part-time job over the years, she had just never been able to get started on the book. She had always kept herself trim and attractive, kept the house well and had been a fascinating companion for Luke but all of her youthful dreams had become secondary to Luke's work needs and to those of their family.

Luke found himself studying Kathryn's hands as he tried to put into words his own desires and long dormant dreams of a life full of travel, excitement and adventure. These hands had always been soft and like velvet to his touch and yet when you turned them palm up and looked closely you saw the lines and the callous under the skin that told of the hard work done over the years by these hands in maintaining a home and the thousand other things that Kathryn had undertaken to benefit both him and their family. The thought occurred to him as he stroked the silky softness of Kathryn's hands that this was some of the hardest work he personally had done in a long time, trying to formulate goals and put the words around his own life desires. The funny thing was, Kathryn had not yet in anyway indicated that she thought this talk after dinner was useless or a waste of time. If anything, she actually seemed excited that they were doing this right now. Her eyes sparkled and she felt soft and so much a woman where her shoulder leaned over against his. She looked at him again with that straightforward way she had that had struck him the first time he had seen her in Meier and Frank's Department Store.

He heard her softly say, "So, Luke, after all of this, what are you going to do with it? Where did these two books you have been showing me come from?"

Until then Luke had acted as though he had found the books in a bookstore and been attracted to them. Now he cautiously explained that a friend he had been talking to about possible employment had given them to him and said they might be helpful to him in determining what he really wanted to do with the rest of his life.

On a whim he laughed and turned to Kathryn as he said, "You know, if I could do anything I wanted I would become a millionaire. No make that a multimillionaire and I would become a philanthropist." Luke's mind flashed back to the big black Mercedes that used to arrive in Tierra Fuerte in Guatemala once each week for the mail.

Luke and Cesar had put together their plan for building the Tierra Fuerte Clinic but had realized that even though they could get volunteer doctors and nurses, volunteer labor to build the building, and donated medicines, drugs and equipment they still needed a certain amount of "seed capital" that neither of them had available. Luke had decided himself one evening he was not going to ask his family and friends back in the States for money. This should be a Guatemalan project as much as possible.

It had been Peggy who had suggested to Luke and Cesar one evening they should consider approaching "El Aleman", the German who lived back in the mountains above Tierra Fuerte. At first Cesar had been adamant that they should not attempt that in anyway. The old German kept to himself. No one knew anything about him. Everyone assumed he escaped from Germany after World War II and like many such fugitives had chosen to live his life in lonely exile in Latin America. As they talked that evening they had all three agreed that "El Aleman" obviously had to have some resources available somewhere. They discussed all the pros and cons of attempting to contact him and could think of no way they could talk with him. It was Luke who had finally come up with the idea that he would write a letter in Spanish to the mysterious man with no reference to his past and outlining exactly what role the clinic would play for the local community.

The next day as Luke wrote the letter he thought the best thing to do was use no salutation and to leave the letter unaddressed with the postmaster to be put into the man's P.O. Box. Later that day when he handed the letter to the postmaster he had thought at first the man would not do it. Then muttering something about "stupid Gringo" he had shrugged and taken the envelope.

Days passed. Then two weeks had passed. One day when Luke went into the Post Office the postmaster handed him a thick brown envelope with only, "Luke, Cuerpo de Paz" written on the front of it.

Luke had rushed back to his room and torn open the envelope. Inside was one untitled white sheet of paper with a very precise message written in English in a very proper ink script:

"This town has been good to me.

I want to give something back to

them. Enclosed are $2,000 Quetzales

for your clinic. Do not ever acknowledge the

receipt of this money to anyone at anytime."

There was no name or signature but folded into the short note were twenty brand new $100 Quetzal notes. More than two thousand dollars in American money! Luke could hardly contain his excitement because $2,000 Quetzales was more than they actually needed to pour the concrete floor and begin the clinic building. Even as he held the money in his hands however he knew that he must honor "El Aleman's" request.

Over the next few weeks as he slowly paid in cash for a bag of nails, a box of bolts, bags of cement and other necessities Cesar looked at him with strange and curious looks but to this day sitting here with Kathryn talking about Jim Rohn he had never told a living soul about the envelope with the two thousand Quetzales. His only reference to the money had always been that it came from an "anonymous donor."

Kathryn rubbed her hand on his leg as she said, "I have always wanted to be a charity and society sponsor but we have never had the extra money for that type of thing. I have always been happy Sweetheart, with what we have had but there have been times on Sunday afternoon after church when I am reading the society section of the newspaper when I have had a pang or two of almost envy that we couldn't have lived a life that gave us more of an opportunity to share something of value with others and with a little more charitable meaning".

"Isn't that something! Those are almost the exact thoughts I have been having the last day or two! But, I also know the people who live those lives are different than I am."

Kathryn leaned away from him, "How do you mean that?"

"Well, you know, I worked while I was in school, no fraternities or anything else. I served two years as a Peace Corps Volunteer and always knew that was important but then we got married and started our family and I just always kind of felt the life you are talking about was never really meant for me."

"Luke, do you think perhaps we should somehow have done something different? You have always had a decent salary but we never seemed to have the ability to help others as some people have done. We have enjoyed our life and I honestly don't know what we might have done differently."

"I remember back to when we met. I had my own little business and I had the home on the river. Fortunately it increased enough in value to get us this house. But I was so proud of my little business. It really hurt to give it up. I guess over the years I let myself believe I was better off letting Tom Simon take the big risks and I was fortunate to have the position with Mt. Hood Land and Cattle that I did. Kathryn, let me ask you something that over the years we have never really talked about in depth. Do you think being a millionaire is OK? Does having that much money really corrupt and change people so they become different?"

Kathryn looked at him with the coquettish smile of a twenty-five year old, pulled up her skirt a little so he could see more of her shapely legs that had always captivated him and said, "Why don't you try it and see?"

Her laugh was warm and flowed around him like a clear brook straight off of Mt. Hood. That laugh had always been his downfall! They turned and slowly kissed a long deep passionate kiss of a truly devoted and lasting love.

As they parted he said, "Do I take this to mean we are through talking?"

They both laughed but she looked into his eyes and said. "There is still the question I asked earlier. What happens now? Where do we go with this? And I suppose I also have to add that we are going to need to have some income pretty soon and how does that fit with all our talk?"

He knew her question was a fair one and yet he really had no answer for her and he certainly did not want to lose this close feeling they had shared all evening. For the first time in several weeks he simply said exactly that to her and was slightly surprised when she smiled at him and said, "I know, I feel exactly the same way."

With that she got up and walked into the kitchen. As he started reading to himself he heard her in the background humming and moving some things around. It was quiet for several minutes and then the scent of her favorite perfume caused him to raise his eyes from the little book by Jim Rohn.

His beautiful Kathryn stood in front of him in a pale blue sheer nightgown that only served to enhance and frame the beauty of her amazing body. She reached out her hand and in barely a whisper said, "I think you have read enough for tonight."

CHAPTER SEVEN

"Surplus wealth is a sacred trust which
its possessor is bound to administer in
his lifetime for the good of the community."

Andrew Carnegie

As Luke drove downtown the next morning to meet Dave at Starbuck's the vision of Kathryn walking ahead of him to their bedroom had been almost impossible to shake. How had he ever been so lucky as to have married such a fantastic creature?

Each week for years Kathryn had prepared small packets of vitamins for each of them to take daily and this morning as he walked up the sidewalk to Starbuck's he was playing with the package in his pocket. It was doubly important now he take anything that would help keep his immune system stronger because as he had mentioned to Dave yesterday, not only did he need to pay bills but his health insurance that he had been able to carry forward from Mt. Hood Land and Cattle was about to run out.

Dave was waiting for him even though he himself was a few minutes early. Dave had a paper open on the table in front of him and as Luke sat his coffee down (which Dave had once again prepaid for him at the counter) he pointed to an article on the front page saying the largest entrepreneurial group in the United States was now people over the age of forty-five who were being downsized or retiring early. As Luke glanced at the article Dave laid another page in front of him and pointed to an article written about local college graduates who were unable to find employment in any field, let alone the one for which they had been trained.

"Do you see how big the market is for someone who can realistically help people learn how to operate their own business and make real money doing it? I work with both of these groups and have people in both of these age groups making over $10,000 per month. It is just a matter of having a goal, having a plan and making the commitment to carry out the plan. How did your evening go, Luke? Have a lot to think about?"

A fleeting vision of sheer pale blue silk pulled tight across Kathryn's hips as she lay back last night waiting for him to join her flooded through Luke's mind as he responded, "I sure did! Kathryn and I talked about that little Jim Rohn book and we wound up having a discussion about our dreams and goals like we haven't had since we were first married."

Dave laughed, "Yes, that is often the effect I have on people. I hope the talk was positive!"

"Oh yes, definitely. But it was also a little scary because I realized that I don't have any true long term goals and when I realized that, then I immediately had the thought I would really like to become a multimillionaire and then be a great philanthropist! That is not my normal type of thought! Here I am very much in need of a job and I'm having these daydreams about becoming a multimillionaire philanthropist!"

Dave paused then said, "Do you feel that way because you are afraid it is too late in your life to develop a new career or is it because you don't really feel you could or should be a millionaire?"

"It's almost like that isn't the type of life I am supposed to lead. All my life I have felt you should have enough to get along but if you really made an excessive amount of money you became, well you know, 'filthy rich.'" As he said it Luke knew deep inside his very being there was something very wrong with the thought itself.

Dave chuckled and asked, "Did you like Tom Simon?"

"Of course. I worked very closely with him for nearly twenty years."

"How well do you think you knew him?"

Luke hesitated as he answered. "Tom was a strange fellow in many ways. He had been married twice and interestingly his second wife was older than he was. But, in all the years I was with Tom he never invited anybody I knew from the office to his home. We all knew where it was but it was like this big plantation outside of the main traffic areas and hard to find if you didn't know the area well. I thought I knew a lot about Tom. But a couple of years before he died Kathryn and I were talking about how we only knew his wife very superficially and his friends and the people he did things with were not from the timber industry. He was wonderful to work for, very generous, but very close mouthed. I knew he was very wealthy but I really don't have any idea how much he was worth."

Dave's response left Luke with even more to think about, "Luke, what would you think if I told you Tom made his first million dollars in a business very similar to the one I am in? He did it in less than eight years and developed a very substantial long term income which allowed him the resources to begin making investments of many different types. His first wife and he were divorced many years ago while Tom still lived on the East Coast. He came to Oregon to start over because he felt he could start here without people hassling him all the time about his past life. He came here with a large amount of cash in the bank, an ongoing income from the business he had built in the East, a brand new car and the desire to build something. Mt. Hood Land and Cattle was an old established family business that had been mismanaged, in fact it had basically become a gypo timber outfit, and their time had run its course and was passing into history. Tom didn't know a Doug Fir from an oak tree but he bought the company for cash and three years later he made a solid profit. That was quite a few years before you came along and by then he had a new wife and family and had developed a very large asset base."

Luke by now was quite puzzled and asked, "How do you know so much about Tom and I don't, even though I was with him almost every day for years?"

"Luke, maybe someday I will tell you the whole story but for right now let's just leave it that my father knew Tom like a brother before he came West. Tom had built a very large people-to-people marketing business when these types of businesses were very young and the government and everybody else thought you were crazy if you were involved with one. Tom was very deeply hurt by his divorce. His wife had left him and because of the circumstances the divorce cost him very little in actual money. He came west just like in the old stories and started over. But, the reason I brought Tom up was twofold."

"First, I don't think even you have any idea how wealthy Tom was. For example, did you know he owned an entire block in downtown San Francisco on Market Street? When he died he still owned three buildings and a fifteen acre plot of undeveloped land in West Virginia where he and his first wife had lived. Tom had been born there and intended to live his whole life in his hometown, but obviously that changed. I could go on and on about the wealth Tom accumulated and developed. He accumulated this wealth so he could support orphanages all over the world. Before the term came into general usage he truly was a Social Entrepreneur."

"The second point is the most important. Tom was able to develop his wealth because he learned several things about money very early in life. Two of those things were The Principle of Delayed Gratification and The Principle of Residual Income. Tom also understood that each of us who has the ability to create wealth then also bears the responsibility to create as much wealth as humanly possible so we can share it and create new ways of working with people who, for whatever reason, do not have those same skills. The sad part of it is that a great many of us grow up feeling just as you said a moment ago. That an excess of wealth, or I would prefer to say Great Abundance, is not exactly evil but it is not morally or ethically proper! Right?"

Luke was nodding his head in agreement realizing that somehow he had missed the opportunity to really know a great man. Luke was also puzzling over the question of why he himself felt about money, or better to say, wealth the way he did? Dave had come very close to describing Luke's own attitudes and they hardly knew each other.

"So, Dave, what does all of this really have to do with my meeting you here this morning? It certainly is not going to help me bring in the money I need next week to pay my bills!"

To which Dave responded. "And how do you know it won't help with that?"

CHAPTER EIGHT

"What lies behind us and what lies before us
are small matters compared to what lies within us."

Ralph Waldo Emerson

"Dave, so much of what you are talking about is so esoteric. I deal in a real world and the real world needs for me to go out and earn real money. Right now ....not down the road several months."

"Luke, that is exactly what I want to help you do. But one of the steps everyone who develops true wealth absolutely must take is to determine why he is developing that wealth and what he is going to do with it. Tom knew exactly what he was going to do with his wealth and consequently building or creating it was not a problem. He simply needed a vehicle to be able to accomplish those established goals. Since you read THINK AND GROW RICH you know that is how Napoleon Hill felt. Do you understand and believe deep down inside of you that you really can achieve whatever your mind can conceive?"

"Consider this. Perhaps one of the reasons, Luke, you have not found the job you think you want is because inside of you, you really want something else. Most people who grow up as Christians hear, "Believe and it shall be given unto you," but do you really believe that? What happens if we truly believe something? Our subconscious mind actually begins to draw us into events and meetings with people and books and teachers who give us the information we need to reach the goal we have told ourselves we want. Think about this: Is it possible I crossed your path when I did to help you achieve Abundance?"

Luke was becoming uncomfortable with the turn the conversation had taken this morning and he wasn't sure quite how to take Dave's last statement.

"Luke, don't worry about it right now. Let's talk about making you some money. Have you actually come up with a number of how much you want next month and what you will need afterward on a monthly basis?"

"Yeh, I have and probably it would be about $2,500 this month and closer to $3,500 next month and then up to about $5,000 per month to get me back to where I can at least cover my monthly bills."

"Luke, if that is what you need and if you will do exactly as I say for the next six months I can help you get there. You have to do the work, no one can or will do it for you."

Luke watched Dave as he thought about his response, "Dave, can I put together enough cash over the next sixty days to get to where you say you can help me make larger amounts of money?"

"Yes, you can. Here is how we will do it. The first thing you need to do is get registered with the company I work with and you buy a business package. With that you get..." Dave continued for the next twenty minutes as he outlined the materials Luke would receive and what Luke would be doing for the first several days. He ended with, "Luke, if all of this seems right to you and you are totally comfortable with it then I want you to put down on this sheet of paper seven names. Preferably they will be people just like yourself who are trying to make something happen with their lives."

He turned a tablet toward Luke and handed him a pen. Luke thought for a moment and wrote down one name. Dave gently prodded him with verbal suggestions and suddenly two, then three names came to him. In a few minutes he had seven names on the tablet.

"Now, Luke, we are going to call these people and get an appointment with them to talk with them about this new partnership you and I have formed."

Dave took a cellphone from his pocket and proceeded to tell Luke exactly what he was to say when making the call. Thirty minutes later Luke and Dave had three appointments for later in the week.

"This is how we will create your first cash flow, Luke. For each one of these people who purchase a business package just like you are doing you will receive $100 as a commission on the supplement products in the package. Over the next two weeks our objective is to sign up five people just like this. That will pay you $500 in commissions. When you have signed up your first five people the company has what we call a "Quick Start Bonus." That is $1,000. Add that to your $500 and you will have $1,500 in commissions. See, in two weeks we are half way to your $2,500! Now, let me stop here for a moment. I get excited and I just kind of roll right on! Have you any questions so far?"

Luke had a thousand questions but was unsure where to begin. His number one question was what was Kathryn going to say? Dave had told him it took five hundred dollars to purchase the Business Starter Package. They would be eating into the money they needed for survival unless he was really careful.

Luke slowly said, "Dave, let me ask you this because this will be Kathryn's first question, what happens if we don't find these people like you are talking about? What do we do then? I need to be able to pay my bills."

"Luke, I understand exactly where you are coming from. I have been there myself, but you will never get out of the box you are in if you don't make up your mind to move on, trust in your decision and then take the risk to step out and move ahead. Don't forget, one of the things I explained before is the company has a full money back guarantee on the money you are going to spend for product in the Business Starter Package. Do you think Tom Simon knew that every venture he went into was absolutely going to work? Of course not! But Tom knew that if the stayed on the path he had set out for himself and if he kept his goals in sight he would eventually get there."

"Luke, that is why forty-five minutes ago I told you the first thing I want you to do, with your wife, is to establish a vision and some goals for what your new business will be and what you will achieve with it. I know you can do this business with my guidance. Right now you have to trust and rely on the fact that I know what I am doing. Let me say right here, the vast majority of people do not succeed in this business. That is because they quit! They start to climb out of their box but they never quite put in enough effort to pull themselves over the edge and out."

As Dave was talking he reached into his briefcase and took out a small booklet. On the front was printed CHANGING YOUR BOX. He said, "Here is a little bit of wisdom that I think you and your wife will find interesting. I don't want you to look at it right now but on the very last page I am going to write which box I think you fit in today. You and Kathryn read this tonight. Talk about it. Decide on where your mind set is right now and then look at the last page and see if it matches what I am writing on that page."

As he spoke he completed the statement he had been writing in the back of the booklet. When he finished he took a small stapler from his bag and carefully stapled the last two pages so what he had written could not be read without removing the staples.

He laughed as he handed the booklet to Luke and said, "There, as soon as you folks have determined where you are, then take out the staples and read what I have written."

"Luke it is decision time. We have set up three appointments so I can help you get started. If you are going to do this we need to get you started with the company."

While he had been saying this he had removed a form from his case and without even asking, he had begun filling in Luke's name. He looked up and said simply, "What's your address, Luke?"

He proceeded to fill out the entire form as Luke gave him his phone number and other information. As he reached the bottom of the page he looked up and asked, "How do you want to pay for this, do you want to write a check or use a credit card?"

Luke responded, "Well, you know Dave, I really like what you are saying but Kathryn and I haven't discussed this at all. Five hundred dollars really takes a chunk out of what we have left. I know five hundred dollars isn't a lot of money to start a business but that five hundred is really important toward paying the bills I have right now. Kathryn and I have always shared any decision like this one."

Dave looked at him thoughtfully, "Luke, if I were offering you a job at $3,000 per month salary would you go talk to Kathryn before you accepted it? Or would you agree to start working with me knowing you were doing the right thing and go ahead with accepting the position?"

"Dave, you and I both know I would accept the job and begin working even though the pay was way lower than I need. But this is different. Kathryn and I have both worked hard to create the little we have and I do want to get started with you, and remember, I made the phone calls but I would not feel right spending such a big piece of what we have left without talking it over with Kathryn."

"Actually, Luke, you just gave me the best answer you could have given me. I appreciate and understand exactly what you are saying so let's do this! You go home and talk with Kathryn. I have found that people who give me an impulsively quick response often really don't do much in building their business later. I have your registration form filled out. You folks look at this from every angle and, most importantly, before you start discussing your new business, read this little booklet together!"

CHAPTER NINE

"None of us has gotten where we are solely by
pulling ourselves up from our own bootstraps.
We got here because somebody bent
down and helped us."

Thurgood Marshall

Luke had called Kathryn shortly after he and Dave parted and told her he would be home early and he needed to be able to talk with her seriously about some new ideas. He parked his car in the driveway and subconsciously realized the lawn needed to be mowed again already. One of the first cutbacks he had made after he lost his job had been in the landscaping service that had maintained their yard for the last several years.

Opening the front door he heard the flowing romantic melody of "Rust On The Moon" by Mihana Souza coming from their stereo. They had met Mihana one night in Honolulu when they wandered into Duc's Bistro looking for a "different" place to have dinner. They had both immediately fallen in love with Mihana's style and her ability to move from traditional Hawaiian music to contemporary jazz. That night she had been singing "Rust On The Moon" as a tribute to her mother, Irmgard Aluhi, who had written the song years before. Over the soft music he heard the click of high heels on the kitchen tile and then quiet, as Kathryn stepped onto the rug in the dining room. As she came through the archway between the dining area and the living room he looked twice at the beautiful vision she made. She had on a brightly colored silk print dress that stopped just short of her knees and it hugged her delightful figure in all the finest places. She twirled on her toes as she came across the room making the skirt and a silk magenta-pink slip stand out away from those glorious legs. He could only stop and thoroughly enjoy the enchanting picture as she swept across the room and into his arms.

Her first words were, "Hi handsome, I like it when you come home early."

She pulled him into the kitchen where she had a fresh pot of coffee made and as she poured them each a cup she said, "Where do we start? Do you want to begin this discussion right away? What happened with Dave this morning?" Wow, Luke thought, here is this gorgeous woman, hair fluffed out all over her shoulders, obviously fresh from her shower, smelling incredibly delicious and she is saying, "Where do we begin."

Luke said to her, "First, let me adjust to this beautiful female that is acting like she just got married and who looks absolutely ravishing."

He kissed her with a new found excitement. As they sipped their coffee and sat at the center counter in the kitchen Luke told her about his talk with Dave and explained as much as he could about Dave's business.

Luke pulled the little booklet from his briefcase and showed it to Kathryn. She read the title: **CHANGING YOUR BOX.**

"Honey, what does this title mean?"

"Dave said that he wanted us to read it together and then talk about it."

With that Luke began to read the one page forward and realized that what it said was exactly what he and Dave had been discussing for the last two mornings.

FORWARD

*This little booklet has been written to help
the thousands of people who started out in
life as I did, with a distorted concept of the
value of money, wealth and abundance.
In writing this booklet I am sharing the steps
in my own growth process that took place
between my personal ages of twenty and
twenty-five. Hopefully the experiences I have
written about here will help many others to
work their way through the confusion that
often exists in many of our minds caused
by early childhood teachings that led
us to believe that money is evil. I am
not an educated man and this is most
probably the only piece that I will ever
write. I write this sincerely and from my
heart in an attempt to save you the time
and extra effort that it took me to learn
how and why I had developed, at an early age,
certain thoughts and ideals that I needed to
change before I could truly gain
Security and come into Abundance.*

Tom Simon

Luke stared at the name in amazement. What? Tom Simon had written a booklet like this? Why had he never heard about it or even seen it?

"Luke, what are you staring at?" asked Kathryn.

Luke held up the booklet for her to see.

"It appears there is a great deal you never knew about your old boss!"

Luke turned the page and saw, "The First Box."

The following four pages described in detail how many people, especially of a strong fundamentalist background, form the concept that hard work is necessary for a good livelihood but that an excess of wealth borders on immorality. Tom Simon described how as a boy he was continually made aware through Sunday School lessons and the Sunday morning service that money was a basic source of evil in the world. And yet as a teenager he saw a great dichotomy within his own church. The leaders of his church were always successful businessmen in the community and they not only provided well for their families lifestyles but also appeared to have accumulated a certain amount of assets or even wealth.

His description of the inhabitants of Box Number One was quite simply that they were people who willingly accepted the status quo and who had a total lack of desire and aspiration for growth or improvement. They were quite content to achieve nothing more than mediocrity. They almost always believed that virtually everything that happened to them in life was someone else's fault. They blamed the government that their taxes were too high. It was their employer's fault they did not make enough money to pay their bills and "get ahead." If only they had received an inheritance from their family the way the people who ran the town did then they could have achieved the same things in their own life. Very seldom did the people in Box Number One ever take the responsibility themselves for the way their lives developed or for their personal lack of Abundance. Those in Box Number One often developed a certain pious religiousness to being low income and impoverished. It made them feel holy. According to Tom these were very often the same people who at one time in his own career had responded to him when he talked with them about the opportunity he was using to build his own personal wealth and Abundance with, "It is fine for you to do that but for me, I am more interested in serving people and helping humanity than I am in making money off of my friends." Did these people not understand there is an ancient axiom that rings true in this modern world more than at any time in past generations: "Poor people can't help poor people."

Luke sat thinking about what he had read and handed the booklet across to Kathryn. She had sat quietly the entire time he had been reading and he had not even realized it.

Kathryn began to read silently, once or twice looking up to study Luke's face. In a few minutes she laid the book down on the counter between them and said, "Well, what do you think?"

Luke's reply was, "I'm not sure what to think."

"Luke, his description is just the way you describe both your childhood church and many of the people you got to know when you lived in Tierra Fuerte in Guatemala."

"I know." said Luke. "Let's see what Box Number Two is all about. Let's read to each other rather than read it by ourselves."

Tom described Box Number Two as being quite different. Luke read two or three pages aloud and then Kathryn took a turn. As they read back and forth they both began to see themselves and their own family as being, at least partially, of a Box Number Two attitude. Tom said most people in Box Number Two had come from a background with a Box Number One poverty mentality. It showed itself over and over in the way people would talk about wanting success, trying to set goals, and wanting to grow through personal development; but every time they would begin to climb out of their box their old ingrained thought patterns regarding an abundance of wealth and money and even success itself would drag them back down into the box with everybody else. Tom described how very difficult it had been for him to leave his early training behind and begin to take concrete steps, like writing down his goals, that would help him climb up and over the edge of Box Number Two. Tom had felt that Box Number Two people had somehow become aware of what was outside of their Box---unlike those in Box Number One who seemed virtually unaware of what possibilities even existed outside their Box. In the description of Box Number Two Tom brought up three principles he felt most people in Box Number Two were aware of and at times even attempted to practice. These were; The Principle of Tithing, The Principle of Residual Income and The Principle of Delayed Gratification. It had been Tom Simon's observation that people who moved out of Box Number Two to Box Number Three began putting these principles into practice even before they started trying to climb out and thus enabled their own ability to climb the wall. Tom's descriptions of these Principles were fairly simple on the surface but obviously for him had been of extreme importance in building his own life of Wealth and Abundance.

As Luke and Kathryn discussed The Three Principles their conversation centered around the way Tom had outlined them himself.

THE PRINCIPLE OF TITHING

The great economic entrepreneurs of history have all seemed to agree that giving back to society in gratitude for what has been given to you is one of the foundation stones for developing both your life and your assets. Many people of religious background and training understand the concept of tithing ten percent as it is outlined in Scripture but once they have given ten percent to the religious institution of their choice they then walk by the beggar on the street. Tom wrote of tithing as being one of the most difficult Principles to understand and definitely one of the most difficult to implement.

The way Tom described The Principle of Tithing went far beyond simply designating ten percent of your income to your local religious institution but went on to include many philanthropic concepts and ideas, as well as a totally different perspective on a tithing percentage based on giving out of love and gratitude as opposed to "tithing" out of an obligation to do so.

THE PRINCIPLE OF RESIDUAL INCOME

Tom stated very clearly in this section he believed by far the majority of people employed every day in the work force traded their time for dollars every one of those days. They did not understand the value and concept of building a base of work accomplished and completed that would be capable of paying an on-going dividend in their future or perhaps even for the rest of their lifetime. That is, they worked for a set amount of money per hour or week for a certain period of time and that created and equaled their daily or weekly income. Their income stops if they do not show up for work. There are many variations of this plan but basically this group includes everyone from medical doctors and teachers to tractor drivers on farms. Tom felt everyone early in life should develop something which would pay them over and over throughout their life for the original work accomplished. He gave a number of examples: an author who writes a book and for years afterward receives royalties as books are sold; insurance salesmen who receive commissions year after year for policies sold one time, composers who receive royalties for songs played months or years after the composition is first published. The residual income Tom had received over the years for the rental price on the properties he owned in West Virginia had paid for the purchase price of the land many times over.

THE PRINCIPLE OF DELAYED GRATIFICATION.

As Tom explained it, The Principle of Delayed Gratification required working hard for a period of time at the start of your plan so that in later years you would draw long term financial benefits from the initial time, energy and money invested. From the end of WWII on into the Fifties and Sixties the growth of IMMEDIATE GRATIFICATION was phenomenal. Television through its' ability to instantly provide news coverage from around the world contributed to this want for immediate gratification. Fast food chains which had not existed in the Forties, by the mid-Sixties were becoming common place as a source of lunch and dinner for people working outside the home. Airplanes could now traverse the North American continent in a matter of hours, whereas only a few short decades before it had taken days by train and only a hundred years before that it took months by wagon. The Principle of Delayed Gratification works just the opposite from the developing trends for instant immediate gratification.

The entire concept centers on the idea that there are some things in life worth taking the time on the front-end to develop properly so that as life progresses we have the opportunity to reap greater benefits from the eventual harvest. Tom used as a principle example of this theory the entire concept of replanting forests for the future use of generations whom the planters of the forests would never even see. College students usually take at least four years to receive their degree. Without even realizing it they are participating in a form of delayed gratification. A football team practices the same plays over and over and each time they refine and improve their execution of the play so that on Saturdays during the season to come they will have given themselves every opportunity possible to walk off the field victorious at the end of the game. A professional photographer will often collect shots of trees or mountains or babies for years so that at some point in the future he will hopefully see his book of photos on sale in bookstores across the country.

As Luke and Kathryn read the descriptions of these three Principles they realized how correct Tom was in his opinion that the majority of people remained in Box Number Two because they would not execute a plan with enough willpower backing it to resist the temptations not to tithe and not to wait for the development of their residual income base. Tom had also written something Luke never forgot over the years to come, "No one likes or enjoys delayed gratification, but winners learn how to use it to their personal advantage."

The section of the booklet about Box Number Three opened with a verse of Scripture:

"Honor the Lord with your wealth,
with the first fruits of all your crops;
then your barns will be filled to overflowing,
and your vats will brim over with new wine."
Proverbs 3:9-10

Tom Simon had acknowledged he began his life as an adopted child in what he had written in the section about Box Number Two and it had been a difficult climb for him to move from Box Number Two to a life of Abundance and Freedom in Box Number Three. He had always wanted to live a life without want or lack but as a youth he struggled with learning how to become a part of the group having "Abundance."

Luke and Kathryn read through the pages about Abundance and Box Number Three. They occasionally stopped and looked at each other or reached out to touch one another. It was as though they both were coming to realize for the first time in each of their separate lives and definitely for the first time in their corporate married life that they each carried within them certain thoughts, fears, ideals and even "accepted truths" that had been holding them back from achieving real Abundance. Abundance according to the way Simon spoke of it was so much more than simply having wealth and yet in a way they apparently had never really understood wealth was virtually a responsibility for those having an Abundant lifestyle. For it was through Abundance people were able to truly be servants to humanity.

Tom Simon told the story in this section about how as a young man he had been in a small group meeting with a very wealthy individual who had made his fortune through a large people-to-people marketing business and he had heard this man say, "Poor people can't help poor people." That short phrase, which he had stated also in the section about Box Number One had lingered in Tom's mind for months until he came to fully understand what it meant when another wealthy acquaintance of his expressed a truth of Abundance to him one night in Chicago. They had been discussing one of the great modern day leaders who constantly through her everyday life attempted to reach and help poor people in Third World countries and Tom had expressed great admiration for what this particular individual had achieved in developing a personal ministry that had reached many thousands of people in India. His friend had listened quietly for several minutes and then had said, "Tom, I appreciate the way you feel, but always remember that she is able to live a life of poverty and still conduct the life and ministry she does because she has many people just like myself who write her foundation very large checks every month."

That night Tom had begun for the first time in his life to realize the full importance of putting behind him forever any thought that the acquisition of excess money or wealth was wrong and to fully devote his energies to the development of a vast fortune with which he could have true Abundance and share with many around the world his good fortune. Luke had never really thought much about an Abundant life before---his attitude had been, "Why should I even be concerned about that? That is way beyond me!" The way Tom Simon wrote about Abundance it was something every person on earth could at least reach for and many who felt it was far beyond their reach would actually attain if they only chose to reach high enough.

To stand quietly on a hill looking out over the vast Pacific Ocean as the sun slowly descends beneath the horizon and the sky goes through a thousand color changes that are forever recorded in your minds eye is to begin to appreciate the length, breadth and the immenseness of Universal Abundance. And most amazingly, the sun will repeat the performance tomorrow evening with a totally different choreography of colors, clouds, birds and memories. Abundance does not mean simply to have enough. Abundance means to have what you need with enough left over to supply a multitude of others also! The shortage of anything; be it money, food, energy or any other desirable item, is in our mind and in our perception of the shortage. If we will study enough and learn as much as possible about faith and our own strengths we will understand this ancient axiom and thus be taking a major step toward moving into Box Number Three and Abundance.

As Luke and Kathryn finished the short booklet they almost involuntarily stood and held each other close. This was truly one of those moments that occurs in life when one person, male or female, regardless of creed, race or religion has a moment of epiphany and is fortunate enough to be able to share it with another fellow human being. They continued to hold each other for several moments as though fearful that if they parted they would somehow break this union that was being forged between them. They recognized the warm feeling flowing between them for what it truly was; renewed hope. Not only renewed hope for their income and future security but also for their continued love and growth together.

Luke brushed Kathryn's hair with his hand as he stepped back to his seat on the stool by the counter and looking at her with both the love of years shared in marriage and this new found emotion of an expanded appreciation of her as an individual. He said, "Kathryn, we have been through a lot over the years. Something is happening here that seems to be different."

She nodded her head but made no comment---only continued to look at him as though waiting to see what was next.

"Have we been given a vision of a path that we are to follow?" Luke said. "Kathryn, I have never really had this type of experience before."

Smiling the gentle smile he loved so much she responded, "Yes, you have Luke, don't you remember how you felt when I was coming down the escalator years ago in Meier and Frank and you looked up at me? I think this moment is perhaps very much like that and we have a responsibility to talk through, right now, what it means."

Luke had been turning back and forth the last two pages of the booklet; the ones Dave had stapled together. Looking at Kathryn he said, "Which box are we in?"

With no hesitation she responded, "Box Number Two, we are on the bottom of the box and the sides are really high! A couple of years ago, if we had been willing to discuss this type of thing then, I would have said that we were part way up the side and trying to get out. Right now I think we are on the very bottom. And you know something, Luke? I feel like we are looking for somebody to put a rope down into the box to help us out when in reality we have to create our own way out starting right where we are, here tonight."

Luke thought about what she had said and then replied, "You may be right, honey. I sure haven't found anything have I? And I really have been looking."

Luke opened a drawer and found a staple puller. He carefully removed the staples Dave had put in earlier in the day. He opened the page and read aloud,

"Luke and Kathryn,
Now you have read about the Boxes. Tom had
a great deal of insight. In my opinion, from
the conversations we have had, you are on the
bottom of Box Number Two hoping that someone

will hand you a ladder down to get out.
No one is going to do that. Fortunately I am
in Box Number Three and I can reach across
to give you encouragement and a helping
hand, but I cannot do it for you.
The two of you, on your own, must now
decide what you will do to climb out of
Box Number Two.
I know you can do it!
Wishing you an Abundant Life!

Dave

"It looks like Dave feels just like you do, Kathryn." Luke mused. "So what do you think we do now?"

"Tell me more about this business of Dave's." was her response.

For the next two hours they talked back and forth as they read the brochures and materials Dave had given to Luke. Luke carefully explained it would take five hundred dollars to purchase their Business Builder Kit and to become registered with the company. Kathryn made another pot of coffee and as it gurgled away and its special aroma drifted through the kitchen Luke could not help but recall how delicious the coffee had always been in Guatemala. It was there he had first experienced "esencia" or coffee essence and had always enjoyed the ritual of pouring the heavy dark brown coffee concentrate into his cup, adding boiling hot water, hot milk and a little sugar to just the taste he enjoyed. Recalling that small ritual made him think of Tom Simon's comments about delayed gratification. Kathryn always made coffee in a percolator. It was easier and much quicker than the other process.

Kathryn poured them each a fresh cup of coffee and reseating herself she leaned back on her stool, looked at her husband and said, "Luke, this is totally uncharacteristic of me to be this impulsive but I feel we should go with Dave. You know, years ago my Grandfather told me as a girl that I should always pay attention to my morning thoughts, because morning thoughts are much wiser than those of the night, and that whenever possible I should take three days to consider or to let my morning intuition guide me in making decisions. My life has not always been such that I could do that. I have told you many times that coming down the escalator years ago, when I looked across the crowd and saw you, I knew without question I was going to marry you and spend my life with you. But, in almost every situation my grandfather has been right about my morning thoughts."

"Do you remember two mornings ago when I wore the black satin nightgown and you got up early to go meet Dave?"

Luke thought to himself, "Of course I remember, I almost didn't leave you!"

Kathryn laughed and Luke realized he had actually said out loud what he had been thinking.

"Luke, I lay there in bed after you left and I went through my morning thoughts and I knew you were supposed to be meeting with Dave that morning. Each day I have been thinking harder in the mornings about what we are supposed to do and each time I come back to this thing about Dave. I have prayed a great deal about this and I am confident we should spend the five hundred dollars and move ahead."

"You and I both profess to believe our God truly works in our lives. Well, I believe we exercise our faith when we make tough decisions. This is a tough decision. We don't have many resources left. But, I believe the decision to get started is like stepping up onto a block of cement at the bottom of Box Number Two and we will be taking a major step toward being able to reach the top of the box."

Luke made arrangements that night to meet Dave the next morning and when he walked into Starbuck's he was surprised to see a young woman sitting at the table with Dave.

"Hi, Luke, how are you this morning? Luke, meet my friend Delores. Dee is also a fairly new person in my business and I wanted you to meet her."

The three of them talked for over an hour and Luke realized quickly that Delores had learned a lot about the products and the company business in a short period of time. Dave also explained in the course of the conversation that if it was agreeable with Luke he was going to place Luke and Kathryn to be directly managed by Delores in his organization. Dave was careful to explain that Luke would still be working directly with him but this was one of the ways he helped his new people get started.

As they prepared to leave Dave looked at Luke and said, "Tomorrow night a friend of mine is going to be in town and he is giving a short talk about what we are all doing in Wellness Marketing. I would really like it, Luke, if you and Kathryn could join us."

As Luke accepted the invitation he realized this was a major step in his and Kathryn's climb out of Box Number Two.

CHAPTER TEN

"Today, there is no better example of
Gods' hand at work, than in the emerging
wellness industry and in the positive economic
forces behind the wellness revolution that
is about to take place."

Paul Zane Pilzer

The following evening Luke and Kathryn arrived early for the meeting and found about ten people already in the room. Dave and his friend were up toward the front. When Dave saw them he motioned for them to join him

"Hello. You must be Kathryn. Your husband refers to you all the time. This is my friend Kenneth Park and I am glad you both will be able to hear him tonight."

With that simple introduction Dave included them as a part of the group and the conversation continued. It seemed several people in the small group had been a part of the business for some time. Delores was there and Luke introduced her and Kathryn as they all turned to take seats near the front. By the time Dave stood at the front of the room to introduce Kenneth there must have been about seventy-five people who had gathered to learn what this was all about.

As Kenneth began his talk Luke knew immediately this was going to be interesting. Kenneth was a good speaker and his subject was one that concerned every person in the room. It was what he called the Wellness Revolution. Kenneth quickly developed a background of need for Wellness or better health worldwide by describing three principal historical events.

First, he discussed briefly the many diseases that had sprung up around the world during the twenty year period beginning about 1975; He mentioned SARS, West Nile Disease, AIDS and the Bird Flu. He then moved to a short but clear presentation about how agricultural growing practices and harvesting methods had changed dramatically in the last half of the Twentieth Century and most of the food being sold through supermarkets and fast food restaurants has very little nutritional value when compared to harvests in the 1940's and 1950's. He concluded the first portion of his talk with an intriguing piece about the growth of the pharmaceutical drug industry, its evolution into an industry guided more by profits than true service to the consumer and how pharmaceutical drugs in the form of antibiotics had been greatly overused for several decades.

Having established a strong need for dramatic change world-wide in healthcare he developed his theme of what he termed The Wellness Revolution. At this point Kenneth had switched from using the term The Wellness Revolution to what he called The Wellness Industry. Luke was fascinated with the way Kenneth described the healthcare system of the twentieth century as really a "sickness care" system and that in 1994 an Act of Congress had passed with no dissenting votes that had been fundamental in giving this Wellness Industry a strong start. He had referred to this piece of legislation as The Dietary Supplement Health and Education Act (DSHEA) and said that, even though many people were unaware of the Act itself, it was affecting every one of their lives. Kenneth said that in fact Paul Zane Pilzer, the famous economist, was predicting that the Wellness Industry would be the next trillion dollar industry. Kenneth presented a compelling story of why everyone needed to be using the nutritional supplements produced by his company. He took about twenty minutes describing them and he explained that his company gave certain individuals the opportunity to develop great wealth through distribution of their supplements but the real satisfaction came from being able to help so many people by improving their own and their family's nutrition. He ended by relating that his company had made a decision early in their development to be involved in working to eradicate certain aspects of poverty in the world and that for every product a customer purchased the company donated a similar nutritional product to malnourished children

Later that night as Luke and Kathryn sat in their kitchen sipping a cup of tea they were both quiet as they thought about everything Kenneth had said. Finally, Kathryn looked up at Luke and said, "Luke, I have this deep down feeling this is where we belong. I don't know very much about nutrition and supplements but what Kenneth was saying about The Wellness Industry made sense to me. Just imagine what it would be like to be able to truly help people who were sick and desperate! All the years I have known you, you have talked about what you have wanted to do for the people where you lived in Tierra Fuerte while you were in the Peace Corps. Mr. Park spoke tonight about how some people become "social entrepreneurs "as they develop their businesses. Luke, you have always been a social entrepreneur all your life, beginning with the Peace Corps. You just never had the right vehicle for creating the business and cash flow that you needed. Think about it.....this may be a vehicle for you to really be of help to that community."

Luke responded, "And get paid for doing it. Kathryn, Tom Simon used to always say a good business deal had to be a win-win situation for everybody involved in it or it was a bad deal. I have to tell you the truth, I actually got excited listening to him tonight but I want us to be cautious."

"Luke, we have been cautious all our lives! We don't want to be foolish, but if we truly are going to move to real Abundance and leave Box Number Two behind forever then we absolutely have to step out on our own new road in the belief our venture is going to be successful. We have been praying for guidance and for something to come into our lives that we could truly make into a success. I think, Luke, like I told you the other night, it is time for us to demonstrate our faith."

CHAPTER ELEVEN

"I find it fascinating that most people plan
their vacations with better care than they
plan their lives. Perhaps that is because
escape is easier than change."

Jim Rohn

Four months had passed since Luke and Kathryn had decided to join in this new Wellness Marketing business with Dave. In that time Kathryn had become a true advocate with Luke in building their business. She had found she enjoyed talking with the people, she was using the products they were selling and she loved how they made her feel. She was even attending regular meetings with Luke so she could continue to learn more.

Kathryn's father had worked in the aviation industry and at one point his former employer had gone through some very serious financial challenges and her father's pension program had very unexpectedly been slashed in half. Kathryn had watched as other large well-known companies had been forced to make budget cuts and even slash back on health insurance program expenses as well as pension program contributions just as had happened with her father. She watched her father as he entered his sixties with no health insurance, no long term care and the pension benefits he had worked years to accumulate nearly wiped out. He had grown reclusive and spent hours by himself puttering in his backyard to the total frustration of her mother who had never expected to have to live hand-to-mouth in their retirement years. Kathryn was constantly on the lookout for ways to broaden and enhance their income sources because of this experience.

Their new business venture was actually growing just as Dave had told Luke it would. Dave kept telling them it was because Luke was doing exactly what he told him to do and Luke and Kathryn believed him. Due to her father's situation Kathryn was also looking for other projects. Not that she was leaving their principal business or putting any less work into it, but she did not want all of their financial eggs to be in one basket.

As a result Luke returned home one evening to hear her say, "Luke, next week there is a seminar down at the Red Lion Motel about developing additional income sources and I think we should go. We may not be totally ready for it but it has to do with creating various streams of income and that sort of thing and we need to be preparing for when we have the money to expand our cash flow."

Luke was not really sure he wanted to take the time. Their little start-up business was succeeding because he stayed focused and put every minute into it. And yet, maybe Kathryn was right and they needed to be looking ahead. He certainly could not complain about the way she was participating in what they had named "K and L Enterprises." She was the one who had taken a special workshop so they would be sure to get all the possible tax advantages of operating a home-based business. There were a lot more tax advantages than he had ever imagined there could be with a small business. Several times she had found someone at the store, church or some obscure place who needed to talk about the products they had available. They now were realizing these products were changing what was happening with many peoples lives. Upon occasion she found someone who was like Luke had been after Mt. Hood Land and Cattle closed and they needed desperately to create a source of income.

Luke agreed that perhaps they should go to the seminar and, marking it in his daytimer, he promptly forgot about it.

The next morning Luke was sitting in Starbuck's going over his personal schedule and thinking about what he might be doing next to add additional creativity to "K and L" as they now referred to their business. He pulled from his briefcase a manual that Dave had given him the first morning when he had met his new sponsor, Delores, and for the hundredth time he looked through it. It contained twelve chapters and was titled:

THE FORTUNE FORMULA

1) CREATE AND BUILD YOUR VISION

2) DEVELOP A PLAN OF ACTION

3) GETTING STARTED

4) PERSONAL GROWTH

5) PROSPECTING

6) ENROLLING

7) BUILDING YOUR ORGANIZATION

8) BUILDING YOUR INTERNATIONAL BUSINESS

9) TRAINING YOUR GROUP

10) RETENTION

11) DEVELOPING YOUR PERSONAL LEADERSHIP SKILLS

12) BIBLIOGRAPHY

Luke felt very fortunate because obviously Dave and his group had taken a great deal of time developing this manual and in putting together this duplicatable plan. There were some questions it did not answer but for the most part Luke had found that if he followed it step-by-step he was becoming successful.

There was no question that his urgency had indeed created his reality and what he and Kathryn had initially developed as their vision was almost exactly what they were building.

He reached for his cellphone and punched in Dave's number. He should ask him about the meeting tomorrow night because he had heard their regular meeting place was being closed for a few days due to a burst water pipe. Dave's voice came onto the phone and Luke knew from the background noise he must be out on the golf course.

Luke asked, "Dave, are you out there again?"

Laughing Dave responded, "Yes, and I just made a beautiful par on the fifth hole. What can I do for you?"

He and Dave talked for a few moments and as they were about to part Dave said, "You know, Luke, you are at a place where you need to play more to build your business. Remember, Work Hard, but Play Harder! That is what makes it all worthwhile!" With that he clicked off and was gone.

Luke finished his coffee thinking about what Dave had said. It sure seemed to work for Dave. Maybe he and Kathryn needed to think about what they could do that would give them the opportunity to play more and build their business at the same time. Perhaps travel, even a cruise to Alaska or the Mediterranean.

The next week went by very fast and before Luke realized it the time had arrived for the financial seminar. He had agreed to meet Kathryn at the Red Lion because he had an appointment in the morning. At one o'clock he parked in the nearly full parking lot and walked in through the big double doors that were the entrance to this elegant hotel on the Columbia River. As he entered he immediately saw his wife on the far side of the lobby talking animatedly with four other women. She had on a dark blue wool suit that fit her perfectly and she had worn a pair of medium height heels with sheer navy blue stockings. He had always told her high heels made her already beautiful legs look even more attractive and frequently when she wore them she would make a point of whispering into his ear when they were in public like this. "Just for you, Sweetheart!" He always appreciated that.

She turned as he walked up behind her and smiled her lovely full face and sparkling eyes smile. He almost caught his breath as he saw how her perfectly proper light blue satin blouse accentuated and defined her amazing figure.

"Hi, Sweetheart, please meet my new friends."

As Kathryn introduced each of them he shook hands and formed, as we all do, his first impressions of each of them. One was not as well dressed as the others. Actually, she may have had the same quality clothes as the other women but she just didn't quite seem to be together. All of them were apparently there to investigate how to broaden their incomes and increase their security. They all continued talking as he looked around the room. Seeing a friend of his from his old Mt. Hood Land and Cattle days he excused himself and went across to say hello.

The seminar was three hours long but was really very interesting and the time went by quickly. Both Luke and Kathryn made several notes about specific things they felt could be important to their own business. Then the afternoon was drawing to a close. Kathryn leaned over and said quietly in his ear, "Do you have anything going or can we stop someplace for a bite to eat and take Julianna with us?"

Luke recognized the name as that of a tall fairly attractive brunette who had been in the group with Kathryn when he first came into the lobby earlier.

"OK by me. Is there a special reason?"

"Yes." responded Kathryn. "She wants to learn more about THE FORTUNE FORMULA and our residual income plan. Since they mentioned residual income here in this meeting I'm sure we can talk with her."

Kathryn stood up and went to find her new friend Julianna. It had always intrigued him how women networked together so easily and quickly whereas men were normally much more reserved and could often sit side by side for hours and do nothing more than exchange perfunctory greetings. Women usually responded to that by saying that men should probably talk more. But, in his experience, he had found that in reality most men did not really have a higher respect for men who aggressively pursued a conversation or small talk, as it was referred to, but actually found those men to be bothersome and did not like or appreciate the invasion of their own space.

When they had first started K and L Enterprises this had been something he had to work on extensively. The really difficult part had been to learn how to start and maintain a conversation with another man without chasing him away. He and Dave had spent a considerable amount of time discussing this and Luke recalled that at one point Dave had commented this was one reason why over 75% of the individuals involved in his Wellness Marketing program were women.

Julianna proved to be an easy and interesting person to converse with and dinner for all of them was an enjoyable experience. She had four children. Luke had been surprised when she told them that for she certainly did not look like the mother of four. Of course, Kathryn did not look like the mother of four either. Julianna had been both divorced and widowed. She was presently single, her children were all grown and she had made it clear she was looking to move on with her life.

Later, at home, Luke and Kathryn agreed their business could be of great benefit to Julianna and that Kathryn would be getting better acquainted with her. That brought them to the point of agreeing these types of workshops or seminars might be a very good place to actually meet future business builders.

CHAPTER TWELVE

"He who sows sparingly will also reap sparingly, and
he who sows bountifully will also reap bountifully."

II Corinthians, 9:6

It hardly seemed possible to Luke it had been over three years since they had formed K and L Enterprises and joined Dave in this amazing Wellness Marketing program. Their business had grown almost exactly as Dave had told them it would.

Luke was always saddened however when he would help someone start their own business, provide them the necessary guidance, even furnishing them a copy of THE FORTUNE FORMULA and they would never catch a full vision of what the business could become for them. He would even include the personal mentoring Dave had taught him to provide and these new people would still quit and say the business didn't work for them.

One afternoon he and Dave had been talking about this issue and Dave had laid down his pen and said, "Luke, this is a growth business and I am not referring to the growth of your income. I am referring to a person's personal growth. People-to-people marketing, as we do, is the only business structure I know of where your income grows in proportion to your personal growth as a person. Oh, sure, there are a few individuals who for a period of time may be unethical or who may not grow personally and their income flourishes, but you know what? In every situation that I have seen with a person like that something always happens to them or their business."

"One reason that K and L Enterprises has grown as it has is because you and Kathryn have grown as people. You continue to grow everyday even now that you have far surpassed your old income and the lifestyle you had with Mt. Hood Land and Cattle. Do you remember how much you and I talked about moving from Box Number Two into Box Number Three? Remember the books you read and workshops you both attended? There were books about becoming a "social entrepreneur" that I suggested you read. Luke, I was so very pleased that you took my suggestions and read those books and articles. I know that you and Kathryn have begun your own project designed around working with orphanages. You are becoming a social entrepreneur in your own right and that is making a difference for you. Luke, those people you are saddened by won't put out that kind of effort! Always remember, you cannot do it for them! Your role is to bring the message, be there as a friend and to always offer encouragement. Sometimes there are ways you can offer a person a boost. Remember the night we were talking about the meeting in Los Angeles you really wanted to go to and you had just paid out all your money on bills?"

Luke's response was quick, "Of course I do! I really could not believe that right there you called and arranged an airline ticket for me and handed me enough money for my expenses for two days."

"And, Luke, you remember what I told you that night?"

"Sure I do. You said, 'Repay me if you want but I would rather you pass it on into your own personal business when you find someone who is really putting the effort into building his or her business.' I have never forgotten that, Dave, and there have been a number of times when we have done exactly the same thing."

"Luke, I was willing to do that because I had a gut feeling you were going to keep on climbing until you got out of Box Number Two and moved on over to Box Number Three. But, there are people out there who haven't been willing to exert that effort. Remember Delores? She was a real nice person. My wife spent hours with her on the phone and in our own home giving her guidance and helping her to understand the business. But, she didn't have time to come to the meetings. She said she didn't like meetings. Well, today she is back selling real estate full-time and I understand it is an uncertain and struggling market. I also hear they have to go to a sales meeting every Monday morning and there are no acceptable excuses for not being there!"

Dave and Luke continued to talk about training Luke's organization and how to move his business to the next level. One of the ways their company supported new business development was through incentive trips. The company sponsored several different incentives each year and one of the trips this year was designed only for Distributors in North America and was based upon how much international business your group developed. Luke and Kathryn had traveled to Germany and Italy twice this past year and had been able to qualify based upon that business volume. Dave had been going on regular trips with the company for several years but for Luke and Kathryn this was the first major trip they had won. They took at least fifteen minutes more discussing what Luke could do to help more of his people qualify for trips when Dave looked at him with a big smile and said, "Well, Luke, you and Kathryn should really enjoy this trip coming up to Hawaii. What is Kathryn saying?"

Luke laughed, "Oh, she has been bubbling over for a month. You know we have never really been able to do much in the way of vacations and she is all excited about going to Maui for a week! She has been getting new clothes and everything. The other night I came home and she greeted me in an incredible black two piece swimsuit that made her look like she was twenty-five again!"

"We are both really excited about this trip. You may not realize this but Samuel, one of my top people, and his wife will be qualified for the trip by next week also. How many people do you think will be there out of your group, Dave?"

"We really aren't sure but it looks like at least thirty. We have always taken our group out to dinner but we may be outgrowing the restaurant we have used in the past!"

Luke had taken a couple of hours early in the contest talking with ten or twelve people across the USA and Canada whom he had considered his special leaders. He had helped them all to develop a plan for encouraging each of their own groups on how to use the contest to build their businesses. His advice had been sound and it had worked. They would be on their way to Maui in about six weeks! For Luke and Kathryn it would be a dream vacation!

CHAPTER THIRTEEN

"A single conversation across the table with a
wise man is worth a month's study of books."

Chinese Proverb

As their flight from Portland landed in Maui they both were like teenagers on one of their first dates. They were nervous. They were excited. They were eager to see who else had qualified for this wonderful trip.

The resort itself was beautiful with grass down to the pale sands washed by waves that rolled in easily and softly. There were friends of theirs in the lobby who had arrived from around the country and they laughed and talked with them easily as they were checked in by the hotel staff.

There were five days of meetings, trips and absolutely delicious meals and both of them enjoyed each moment to the fullest. When they had first come into their room Kathryn had immediately thrown open their lanai doors so that the sounds of the waves blew in across the room. She had turned and pulled him into her arms with a long slow passionate kiss and looking up at him with all the playfulness of the truly beautiful woman she was, had said, "Let's enjoy this room to the fullest."

There was a large very comfortable hammock hung across their patio and each afternoon they had made a ritual of sharing an hour lying together in the hammock talking about the meetings they were attending and how they might use the information in growing their own business. Twice they had both fallen asleep holding hands in the warm afternoon sun.

Lying there in the hammock one afternoon Luke's thoughts had turned to the path he and Kathryn had followed to be enjoying the wonderful ambiance of this beautiful resort. Moving from Box Number Two to Box Number Three had been a difficult and arduous task for both of them. Several times they had felt they were making progress and something would happen that would drag them back down to a place where they would feel discouraged, afraid and so very unsure of themselves. Fortunately they were both reading more and attempting, each in their own way, to grow as individuals. Each time one of them felt low the other would have the strength or enthusiasm to somehow lift the low one up. They would look up the side of the Box, look at each other and start climbing again.

One of those occasions had happened about a year into building their business. Kathryn had gone to Minnesota to visit one of her three sisters. Luke had stayed home to try and get in some extra time making calls and some reading that he wanted to get caught up on. Kathryn had been gone about three days. One evening after they had talked on the phone Luke became very depressed and worried about why their business wasn't growing faster. In addition he missed Kathryn. They always tried to travel together and he missed her companionship and the warmth of her loving hugs. Kathryn would be coming home in four days and he had many things to do in that time. Most importantly, he had to get out of this strange "funk" that had taken him over this evening.

That night he struggled to sleep and finally, well past midnight, he drifted off into a strange dreamland that certainly did not make him feel refreshed when he awoke. He met with Dave for lunch the following day and that definitely helped. Dave was one of the most upbeat and optimistic people Luke had ever known and lunch with him was usually a very uplifting experience. By the time Kathryn was due to leave Minnesota he had managed to regain most of his own enthusiasm and joy out of talking with people about their growing business.

He spoke with Kathryn on the morning she was due to come home and they agreed she would call him on her short layover in Denver where she would be changing planes. As the time passed when she should have called he began to wonder what was happening. The hour arrived when she was due to leave Denver and he still had not heard from her. Should he head for the airport expecting to meet her or should he stay at home until she called? Finally he decided he would go to the airport and be there at the time they had agreed on earlier.

As he sat in their car at the airport holding area waiting for her to call him when she got off the plane he thought back over the last three hours. He had checked with the airline and her flight from Minneapolis had arrived on time. In the same fashion her flight leaving Denver had departed on time. That would mean that his phone should be ringing at any moment. Right then his phone rang and Kathryn's voice poured out, clear, excited and bubbly.

"Darling, are you here waiting for me?"

"Kathryn, I am right outside. Tell me where you will be and I will come to meet you."

"O.K. I will be at Baggage Carousel 5 and I have someone with me. We are going to give her a ride home. It won't be too far out of our way. Is that going to be a problem?"

As Luke clicked off his connection with her he chuckled to himself. How very typical of Kathryn that she would have met someone on the airplane and would want to give them a ride home from the airport. He walked across the beautiful covered walkway from the parking garage to the Main Terminal itself and marveled, as he had many times, at how beautiful the architect had made this entry into the City of Roses.

Coming off the elevator on the baggage level he immediately saw Kathryn and began to move swiftly toward her. She rushed into his arms and he crushed her to him. He felt her return his eager kiss. He experienced that same rush of feeling that overwhelmed him each time they were apart for any length of time at all. It was always wonderful to feel her warm passionate body close within his arms. As she pulled away from him she turned in his arms to introduce him to a young Afro-American woman who had been standing to one side quietly observing their enthusiastic reunion.

"Luke, this is my new friend Jennifer. Jennifer, this is my Luke."

Jennifer chuckled good naturedly as she said, "I should hope so! If you were giving that kiss to anyone else I'm not sure I would accept that ride home."

They all laughed as Kathryn explained to Luke that Jennifer had been seated next to her all the way from Minneapolis and they had to move their own bags from one terminal to another in Denver. That was why she had not called from Denver. Jennifer had just recently been discharged from the Army and had been visiting her brother and sister-in-law in Minneapolis. Her husband, Enrico, was still in the Army and was scheduled to get out in about six months.

As they accumulated their bags and settled into the car for the ride to Jennifer's house she and Kathryn continued a quick and easy conversation that obviously must have begun the moment they met in Minneapolis. Jennifer and Enrico had purchased a home in Portland about three years before. They had both been on leave and spent their leave time in the city. They had seen the little house and Enrico's parents were looking for a place to live. It seemed perfect for them to buy the house and for his parents to live there until they both got out of the Army. Now Jennifer was coming home and even though there was an extra bedroom that she would be using she expressed concern about the living arrangements. She was moving into a house that she and Enrico owned but had become her in-laws "home."

Lying here in the hammock in Maui Luke knew that he had never anticipated Enrico and Jennifer would become such an important part of their growing business

As they had driven home from dropping Jennifer off Kathryn had told Luke she had not explained hardly anything about their business to Jennifer but she knew that Jennifer could use what they had to offer. One of the things Luke and Kathryn both had come to understand was that the more help they gave someone else the more their own lives had been enhanced. Jennifer had come out of the military with very few marketable skills. She had been unable to find a job other than one at a local department store as a clerk. After returning home, Kathryn and Jennifer had talked with each other on a regular basis and about three months after they had met Jennifer asked Kathryn what was really involved in their business and if anybody could do it. Kathryn had very carefully shared with Jennifer information about how their business worked and what the concept of residual income really meant. It had taken Jennifer only two days, after watching a corporate DVD, to ask Kathryn if she could meet with her and Luke and start a business of her own.

Luke and Kathryn had developed the habit of giving everyone they personally sponsored a copy of CHANGING YOUR BOX and asking them to read it as the first step in developing goals and an action plan for their new business. People had responded well to the booklet. Jennifer had done the same. Luke had started working and counseling more with her directly himself and when Enrico came home he and Luke had immediately liked each other.

In their first meeting Enrico had looked at Luke and said, "What is the most important thing to do if I want to build a business like the one you are building?" Without hesitation Luke had replied, "Developing relationships. That is what will make your business grow, and besides even if you don't help someone build a business of their own you may well develop a new friend and isn't that what life is really all about?" Enrico had said nothing, looked at him for several moments and then nodded his head slowly. With no more fanfare than that Enrico had joined Jennifer in building their own new business.

Luke and Enrico began having a regular cup of coffee at the same Starbucks where Luke had originally met with Dave and one afternoon Enrico said to Luke, "Jennifer and I have different types of backgrounds and I need to ask you a question or advice or something. Jennifer can trace her heritage back at least five generations. I'm different. I don't even know who my father was and I grew up living with my mother part of the time and my aunt part of the time. I never talk about it but in my first two months in combat I lost part of my right foot and have a piece of bone missing from my kneecap." Enrico had laughed and said, "I carry an official affidavit for when I go through metal detectors because of a small plate here on the right side of my skull. None of that really bothers me but it has seemed to bother any potential employer I have had. I have read your little book about the Boxes but frankly it doesn't all make sense to me. Jennifer says we are in Box Number Two. I'm not sure she is right, maybe she is but I think I am in Box Number One. What should I do? Where do I begin? I know our business seems to be growing but I think I need to do something else to really get it moving like I see other people like yourself doing."

Luke stirred his coffee for a moment then said, "Enrico, I don't know if you are in Box Number One but you already know you want true Abundance. I think you are moving toward Box Number Two but it is going to take a lot of work to get up to where Jennifer is in Box Number Two. Does that make sense?"

Enrico had slowly nodded his head in agreement but he still had a questioning look on his face.

In response to Enrico's look, Luke said, "I gave Jennifer a copy of a book called THINK AND GROW RICH. Have you read it?"

"No, I saw it on the desk but I honestly haven't even looked through it."

Luke responded, "Then that is where we will begin. I had never read it either until I met Dave. I want you to start today and read it. I want you to write down any questions that you have as you read it so that we can discuss them."

Enrico had read THINK AND GROW RICH in less than a week and that had begun a new way of thinking for him. He came to each coffee session with questions and as he grew his business began to grow also. Luke often thought during this time of what Dave had said to him about this being a growth business and it was the only kind of business he had ever seen where your business grew almost in direct proportion to how you grew in your personal life.

There was one incident on the second night that Luke and Kathryn were on Maui which they often mentioned to each other over the years to come. About a dozen of them had gone to a very nice restaurant away from the resort and were sitting around a large semi-circular table enjoying the ambiance of the warm evening, the fading sun on the ocean waves and the friendly conversation. One of the highest income earners with the company was there and in the middle of the meal he asked for everyone's attention and as they quieted to listen he asked, "Do you know who is not here with us?" No one answered as they looked at each other with questions in their eyes and he then answered his own question with, "All those people who told us "no" and who thought they didn't have enough time or some other excuse." Everyone had laughed but it was true. Luke often thought how much so many of those people were missing out on.

One evening as they had quietly finished dinner by themselves a couple they had met the first day asked if they could join them for a cup of coffee. They agreed even though both of them had been enjoying the time alone.

At one point the man turned to Luke and said, "Would you mind sharing a little with us about the Box Number Two and Box Number Three idea? We have developed a pretty decent income and we worked really hard to be here on this trip but somebody we were talking with last night suggested you might be able to help us with a challenge we have. You see, we have become very uncomfortable with having as much money available as we have today and we both feel very strange checking into this hotel where our room costs more each night than a lot of people make in a week or even a month! They said we should ask you about the Three Boxes and some new idea of yours that he called The Quantum Abundance Theory."

Luke looked over at Kathryn who had reached out to touch the younger woman's hand, as he responded, "First let me ask you something. Do you feel guilty about making the kind of money you are making now? If that is true, then have you ever tried to figure out why you feel that way?"

The younger man, whose name was Albert, looked a little confused but replied, "You know Luke, I do feel a little bit guilty but I honestly haven't tried to figure out why I feel that way."

Over the next two hours, as the sun set in yellow splendor out behind the distant sea and other contest winners walked in and out of the ocean side restaurant lounge, Luke and Kathryn explained the journey they had made and in fact were still making along the road to a true understanding of Abundance. They talked about their own rather conservative upbringings and explained the concept of Boxes, One, Two, and Three. Luke also outlined briefly for Albert the concept, first expressed by Kathryn, that they were calling "The Quantum Abundance Theory." Kathryn's idea had been that in order for people to truly understand how to achieve Abundance there needed to be a good definition of Abundance that was measurable and so she had created this new title. They had both liked the idea so much that they were in the process of developing an entire new training program for their group which they had titled "The Quantum Abundance Workshop."

They had designed The Quantum Abundance Workshop so that it explained in detail the entire concept of becoming a social entrepreneur and the importance of giving back to those less fortunate than they themselves a part of what they were gaining. Tom Simon's booklet had stated that one of the most important principles of success was The Principle of Tithing. The concept of becoming a social entrepreneur had gained recognition after Tom Simon had written his small pamphlet but to Luke and Kathryn it was such an important part of why Luke had joined the Peace Corps and it was so aligned with their own desire to be of service to others that they had made it a major part of The Quantum Abundance Workshop.

Often one or the other of the younger couple would nod his or her head in agreement or would ask a question somewhat tentatively as though fearing they might be asking something that would seem naively inappropriate.

Luke and Kathryn had experienced this several times with other couples and were always pleased Dave had taken the time in the beginning to help them understand what Abundance could mean in their own lives.

CHAPTER FOURTEEN

"Imagination is your most powerful faculty.
Imagine what is lovely and of good report.
You are what you imagine yourself to be."

Joseph Murphy, Ph.D., D.D.

Luke looked down at Kathryn with the same wonder and awe he had felt since that day so many years ago beneath the clock in the Meier and Frank Department Store. His wife was the most beautiful and enchanting woman he had ever known. Tonight for receiving this very special recognition as a Platinum Crown Distributor she had selected a platinum colored satin dress that accentuated each curve of her magnificently beautiful body. Her black hair was brushed out long and fell around her face in ebony waves. As always her eyes were her most striking feature and tonight they sparkled and shone with the brilliance of the sun on the snow of his beloved Mt. Hood.

Turning to the crowd he looked out through the bright stage lights and could see in the very front row several of the many people who had been responsible for them being here tonight. There were Samuel Evans and his wife. Samuel had been the first person Luke sponsored eight years ago in the second presentation Dave had made for him.

As their Sponsors, Dave and his wife were in the special receiving line on the opposite side of the stage.

Luke looked at the timing clock on the front of the stage and saw that fifteen seconds of their twelve minute stage time had already ticked away. There was a small console set at floor level on each side of the stage so the speakers on stage could see how much time they had left but the audience could only see what appeared to be a black speaker box. It had always amazed him how quickly the time flew by when you were at the speaker's podium.

Because he and Kathryn had literally built their business together they had agreed to split the time evenly with six minutes for each of them. They had also agreed that she would use her six minutes to talk about "Quantum Abundance and How To Achieve It." He would use his time to tell about the value and importance of visualization in achieving your goals. As she ended her part Kathryn used a quote from their friend Sam Caster, "Everybody has to have a way to make a living. We are blessed to do this."

Luke had given this speech so many times to himself over the past year he did not even look at his notes as he began after Kathryn had completed her section.

"I have given this talk five hundred times this year. I have given it when I was in my car by myself driving to a presentation. I have given parts of it over and over to the walls of my shower in the morning. But most of all I have given this talk to the trees and bushes along a trail that I like to walk near our home in Oregon. I share this with you because what I want to talk with you about this evening is the importance of visualization. Some of you have been to the workshops and seminars Kathryn and I have presented around the world over the past eight years on setting and attaining goals. You know we mention visualization as an important part of developing your business. To me, visualization; the development in our minds of pictures of what we want to achieve, is an incredibly important step that many of us ignore or, because it may be a little scary to us, we do not practice it."

"The finest athletes in the world all practice visualization. Stop and think for a minute, who are the people you enjoy the most as public speakers? Aren't they the speakers who can build word pictures and paint for you a beautiful picture of what their story is about? Of course! One of the greatest users of parables or stories of all time was Jesus Christ. Do you think he used stories by accident? Of course not, he understood the power of visualization in the human mind."

'By delivering this talk to the trees and bushes along that trail in Oregon I created a visual image of myself standing here in front of you that my subconscious mind then began to achieve for me. Now for some of you that may be a little bit weird or far out. Follow closely what I am going to say right now!"

"Everyone of you uses visualization everyday and you simply do not realize it! For those of you who are married, do you remember the first days, weeks and months after you met the person who would become your partner or spouse? Do you remember daydreaming about them? Do you remember how so very many things that happened with you each day would bring your beloved's image to your mind? You probably woke up at night and realized you had been dreaming about what it would feel like to hold him or her in your arms---I know I used to dream about burying my face in Kathryn's beautiful black hair! I could even smell the perfume she wore! Right guys?!"

"Folks, those are all forms of visualization and when we do that our subconscious mind then begins to create ways for us to achieve those things that we are visualizing. The key to achievement then is setting goals for what we want to achieve and learning to visualize the attainment of those goals." Luke had continued for a few minutes giving examples of visualization techniques and his personal thoughts on why visualization works as it does.

"In closing I want to share with you a short quote from one of my favorite books, THINK AND GROW RICH by Napoleon Hill.

"Life is a checkerboard and the player opposite you is time. If you hesitate before moving, or neglect to move promptly, your men will be wiped off the board by time. You are playing against a partner who will not tolerate indecision!

Previously you may have had a logical excuse for not having forced life to come through with whatever you asked, but that alibi is now obsolete, because you are in possession of the Master Key that unlocks the door to life's bountiful riches.

The Master Key is intangible, but it is powerful! It is the privilege of creating, *in your own mind,* a burning desire for a definite form of riches. There is no penalty for the use of the Key, but there is a price you must pay if you do not use it. The price is failure. There is a reward of stupendous proportions if you put the Key to use. It is the satisfaction that comes to all who *conquer self and force life to pay whatever is asked.*

The reward is worthy of your effort. Will you make the start and be convinced?"

CHAPTER FIFTEEN

"Success is the gift we give ourselves,
when we feel that we deserve it."

Kathleen Peters

Once again Luke's pipe had gone out. Only this time he saw he had been daydreaming for well over an hour. He must have had a little awareness of what was going on around him because his lemonade glass on the table was empty.

Apparently the family had begun to arrive because two of their grand-children were playing on the lawn that he had mowed earlier in the morning. They were laughing and running from one end of the large side yard to the other while the big black German Shepherd that was Kathryn's pseudo son chased them back and forth.

Life for Luke and Kathryn had reached a point of true Quantum Abundance and they rejoiced in it. They still actively operated their business that had created their wealth and most importantly gave birth to their large monthly residual income but now they spent most of their time conducting specialized training programs for their own leadership around the world. Their newest training program on The Quantum Abundance Theory had in fact become so popular they now were providing it for private corporations, universities and churches all over the world.

The Quantum Abundance Workshop taught people not only what it truly meant to be a social entrepreneur in today's world but also taught about the Three Boxes and the development of an Abundant lifestyle.

Luke presented the section on entrepreneurship and what it meant to be a social entrepreneur along with all of the things that had to do with using goals and visualization. Kathryn followed with what an Abundant Lifestyle really is with very specific steps as to how to achieve true Quantum Abundance.

The Quantum Abundance Workshop had come about because one day in one of their leadership seminars they had both started sharing with the seminar participants their views on how to change your Boxes, how to grow personally and what it truly means to develop Abundance through being an entrepreneur.

Kathryn had shared with the group that afternoon what she termed, "Moments of Grace." She shared with their students how very difficult it had been for her personally as Luke was attempting to find work and then, after meeting Dave, beginning to use The Fortune Formula program for building their own business.

As she talked about the times that she had sat in their kitchen and cried as she prayed that God would guide Luke to some income source it was obvious to every person in the room that she had experienced all of the anguish, fear and apprehension that each of them was experiencing. Kathryn that afternoon had shown so much passion and quiet strength that later that evening Luke had told her they absolutely needed to develop a special workshop built around what she had said that day. It would explain all the essential points of being responsible, as an entrepreneur, for developing your personal destiny. Because they were seeing so much happen with their own growth since they had begun to develop the concept of being a social entrepreneur they obviously included this in the workshop. In addition, it would combine what they already shared as Quantum Abundance with Kathryn's passionate statement about "Moments of Grace."

Kathryn had looked at him and said, "Luke, do you realize how many times I watched you come home beaten down by your own anxieties and depression over what had happened with Mt. Hood Land and Cattle and I was able not to say anything? Just give you a soft kiss and have dinner ready. There were times I wanted to scream at what was happening to you, most of all what was happening to us, but through what I am terming "Moments of Grace" I was simply there for you and our marriage. Luke, I did not have the strength to do that on my own. I drew strength from the very core of my being in those times and that is what we need to teach people. To have hope and to keep moving forward. That God and the Universe itself will provide "Moments of Grace."

They traveled now only at their own choice and in a much more limited way than they had during the years when they were building what was now a business literally spanning the globe and operating in over fifty countries.

He heard Kathryn in the house and he stood and walked into the warmly colored comfortable living room that six years ago they had redesigned. The stone fireplace with a hearth just the right height for sitting on comfortably was to the right as he came in the door. Even though it was a beautiful warm day outside he and Kathryn both loved and enjoyed a fire so much that almost every morning when they were here at the beach house he built a fire that kept the room warm and left it with just the faintest hint of the delicious aroma of wood smoke. Kathryn had spent many hours selecting the furnishings in this spacious room they now used for everything from small intimate family gatherings to much larger events where they could easily host seventy or eighty guests for one of their numerous business or social functions. Even though their house back in the Valley was larger they both enjoyed the beach house so much that they often chose to gather their leaders here rather than in the more conveniently located house back near Portland. It continued to amaze Luke how Kathryn could make hosting a family gathering or a fundraiser for a local orchestra appear to be done with so much apparent ease. He walked through the living room and the comfortably elegant dining room into the warm inviting kitchen where he smelled apple pie baking in the oven. Kathryn was always wonderful in the way she prepared his favorite foods but he especially looked forward to the times when their family would be here for a meal or a brief stay because that always meant she would bake at least one of those enormous fresh apple pies that were definitely her specialty.

The house had become their heart home as they gathered into it mementos from their many appearances around the world. He took down a fresh glass and poured it half full of the orange flavored lemonade that he prepared regularly and kept in the refrigerator. As he put the pitcher back he saw he would have to make more later today since the grandchildren liked it as well as he did.

Glass in hand he headed into one of his most favorite rooms in the beach house, his den. He had furnished it himself and when they had redone the log house to bring it up to modern living conditions Kathryn had agreed that if she could take one of the former bedrooms and turn it into her own private reading room and art studio then he could take one and turn it into a den. It had cost a pretty penny but his den was just as he had always wanted. A fireplace with a painting of Kathryn hanging over it was toward the back wall of the house. The fireplace was of old weathered stone and on cool days when he worked here he almost always would light a crackling fire. The painting above the fireplace was one that he had commissioned a local artist to paint from a photograph taken of Kathryn on the night six years ago when they had become only the sixth distributor business in company history to become Platinum Crown Distributors.

That night Kathryn had looked more beautiful than he had ever seen her before. Her black hair shone with a luster that had taken his breath away. The satin platinum dress she had worn that night had fit her so perfectly many commented it must have been designed just for her. And, in fact, it had been. The artist painted the background in just the perfect shade of gray with tints of lavender so the entire picture of Kathryn stood out gloriously from the painting. Luke marveled every time he looked at the painting at how well the artist had captured the glow and sparkle in her eyes and face.

Luke remembered the day he had hung it over the fireplace. Kathryn had not known he was having it painted and in fact she had been reminding him regularly that he needed to pick out something to hang above "his" fireplace. When she walked into the den late in the day to tell him dinner was ready she had seen the four-foot-tall portrait for the first time and when she turned from it to him at his desk tears had formed in her eyes. At that moment she had been even more beautiful than the painting.

The den held many remembrances from their travels and various forms of recognition hung on the wall next to the fireplace with one framed letter that he had always kept in a place of honor. It was a personally signed letter from Vice-President Hubert Humphrey congratulating him on having completed his term of service in the Peace Corps. There was also one tapestry that had always held a special place in Luke's heart and it had always hung in a prominent position in either his past offices or his den.

About three feet wide and seven feet long it was a wall hanging with a black background and bright colorful embroidery work on each end. Woven into the end piece at both the top and the bottom was a bright green long tailed Quetzal bird with a scarlet red breast. A weaver in Tierra Fuerte, who made tapestries to sell in Guatemala City, had made it especially for him as a gift after he and Cesar had opened the medical clinic. He had always regarded it as one of the most beautiful gifts he had ever received.

On the opposite wall centered between two windows hung a piece of embroidery Kathryn had presented to him over a decade ago as they had been working to build their business. It was a quotation from a friend of hers who had lived and worked in Ridgewood, New Jersey as Kathryn grew into womanhood.

"The road to success is constantly

under construction, as you are laying

the pavement trust that the road will

wind towards home."

Elaine Bartlett

Around the room were displayed awards and gifts from the numerous trips they now made on a regular basis back and forth to the six orphanages they had formed in Guatemala and three other countries. Very few people understood the significance of the name of the foundation they had created to operate the orphanages; Cuerpo de Paz de los Niño's (Peace Corps of the Children) At first the Peace Corps had said, "No way!" But, as he had fully explained why he wanted the name, what it meant to him and most importantly, that it would be all his own money they had agreed to give him the special right to use the name.

An hour later after having made several calls to his leadership around the world he decided to take a shower and change his clothes before dinner. He walked down the hall and stepped into his favorite room in the beach house.

Their bedroom suite was far larger than most people's living rooms. When they had expanded the house several years before to make room for their growing family they had both agreed this was to be "their" room. It was the one private room in the house. The grandchildren knew they were welcome to come and find them here but no one else was ever invited into this very special area that had become his and Kathryn's own private retreat and sanctuary. They had agreed they would spend whatever was necessary to make it exactly what they wanted it to be.

On one outside wall was an eight foot fireplace with a wide mantel where Kathryn displayed pictures of their family from over the years. The fireplace was the first thing they had mutually decided must be a part of their bedroom. They could lie at night in the huge oversized king bed and fall asleep listening to the river with the light of the fire in the fireplace flickering off the walls of the room.

Kathryn had a large walk-in closet on one side of the room and he had an equally spacious one on the opposite side. The bath with a giant double shower and oversize tub faced a full wall mirror over two wash basins. On the mirror, high up in the right hand corner, Kathryn had placed a small piece of paper with the one word, "**FOCUS,**" written on it in large letters. Kathryn had a whole section in one of her training programs about that one word. She said, "The word Focus is an amazing word. It can apply to any area of your life you need to focus on at that time and hanging that word on your bathroom mirror brings you back into alignment with what you need to Focus on each time you wash your hands." The washbasins below the mirror were far enough apart for them not to bump into each other but close enough to talk and laugh as they prepared for the day.

As Luke left their bedroom retreat after taking his shower he thought back over the many people they had come to know over the past decade and realized for the hundredth time just how very fortunate they had been to meet Dave and to learn the true meaning of Wealth and Abundance. Walking down the hall he stopped at a picture of the first orphanage they had formed in Guatemala.

That first orphanage had been one of his goals and dreams from the time they first started their own business. They had been told by a company leader that if they really wanted to achieve great things with their business then they needed to have a goal that was bigger than just their own personal material possessions. They had taken that advice to heart and because of Luke's own childhood experience as an orphan they had easily agreed that they would develop an orphanage as quickly as possible. It was the amount of help to others they were able to share that had really brought them to a full understanding of Tom Simon's concept of Abundance that years before Dave had shared with them in the little booklet they had read together that evening in their kitchen.

Luke stepped into the kitchen and slipped the Invitation to the Peace Corps Fiftieth Anniversary Celebration into a drawer in the small walnut desk Kathryn kept against a wall across from the sink. He would take it out again on Monday when the family was all on their way back to their separate homes and he and Kathryn would decide how many days they would stay in Washington, D.C. On cross country trips they usually took several days more than their trip required so they could see new sights and visit old friends. It would be interesting to see how many from Guatemala I would be there in Washington, D.C. for the celebration! So many memories from a half century ago!

EPILOGUE

"Now the trumpet summons us again---
not as a call to arms, though arms
we need---not as a call to battle,
though embattled we are---but a call
to bear the burden of a long twilight
struggle year in and year out, 'rejoicing
in hope, patient in tribulation'---
a struggle against the common enemies of man:
tyranny, poverty, disease and war itself."

John Fitzgerald Kennedy

The Fiftieth Anniversary Celebration of the Peace Corps had been an amazing experience! There had been so many activities during the week and the time had passed so swiftly that Luke and Kathryn could hardly believe an entire week had passed.

In reality the activities had started several months earlier when local chapters of the National Peace Corps Association began to hold special events in their own local cities for Returned Peace Corps Volunteers. There had been one in Portland, Oregon hosted by The Columbia River Peace Corps Association which Luke and Kathryn had attended. It had been low key but very nice one Sunday afternoon at the local art museum in Downtown Portland.

Kathryn had urged Luke to attend and participate in every possible function held for the Celebration and Luke would always be pleased they had made that decision.

The first major event they had attended had been the special University of Michigan reception and the gathering on the Student Union steps in Ann Arbor, Michigan for official recognition of the speech made by Presidential candidate John F. Kennedy that gave eventual birth to the Peace Corps. It had been both a somber and a joyous occasion as various public officials and Caroline Kennedy acknowledged the impact of that speech.

Luke and Kathryn had easily agreed that in the Spring of 2011, six months before the actual Celebration in Washington, D.C. they would also attend the Kennedy Library Reception in Boston, Massachusetts. What an affair it had been! Kathryn had at one point whispered to Luke that every possible living relative of both John Kennedy and Sargent Schriver must be there for the event. It definitely was history in the making itself and they both had been pleased they attended.

There were hundreds of small events they obviously could not take the time or the expense to attend but suddenly the September, 2011 Fiftieth Anniversary dates were upon them and they had flown to Washington, D.C. There had been a special reception put together for all Peace Corps Volunteers who had served in Guatemala that was the first event they attended.

Ten out of the original twenty-seven Guatemala I Volunteers had actually attended the Anniversary Celebration. There were many other Returned Volunteers who had been part of subsequent groups in Guatemala and Luke enjoyed getting to know some of those who had followed in his groups footsteps.

Peggy was one of the ten and it had been wonderful to see her and to meet her husband. They had been married for over thirty years and had raised three sons two of whom were now off raising their own families. The third son had just completed the first year of his two year term as a Peace Corps Volunteer. Peggy and Kathryn had liked each other immediately and for the rest of the official four day event they spent hours together learning about each other. Peggy's husband, James, had recently retired as an airline captain and was quiet by nature.

The walk across The Memorial Bridge that crosses the Potomac with all of the host country flags flapping in the breeze had been a colorfully exciting time. Only four of the Guatemala I Volunteers actually made the walk but Luke and Peggy enjoyed immensely the time they had together crossing the river and reminiscing about their time in Tierra Fuerte.

It had been a quietly somber group that had gathered at President Kennedy's grave site in Arlington National Cemetery for a special wreath laying ceremony on the second afternoon of the Celebration. Luke could not help but remember that November afternoon in 1963. He and Cesar had gone into Guatemala City to pick up cement for the clinic floor and as they were loading the sacks into his Jeep one of the salesmen had come running out shouting, "Your President Kennedy has been shot! You must go back to your village right now!"

They had left immediately and later that night back in Tierra Fuerte, having gone down to the local tienda they had listened to the British Broadcasting Corporation's shortwave broadcast with about twenty villagers. He would never forget the somberness of the group that night. Within days pictures of President Kennedy began to appear in tiendas, bars and on the walls in people's homes often beside a picture of the Pope or a saint. To them John Kennedy was a hero. Not only had the Peace Corps come because of him but The Alliance for Progress and many other programs that directly related to the way they lived were seen as coming to them because of him. On top of that he was a Catholic and was married to "Jackie" whom they regarded as the ideal wife and woman.

The entire Fiftieth Anniversary had been designed as an attempt to recapture in some way the tremendous feeling of pride and service President Kennedy had brought out in so many of those first Volunteers.

The major Anniversary Event had been attended by the President and his wife. The President had given a stirringly patriotic speech to the large throng that had gathered. He had even at one place in the program moved down into the crowd and, much to the consternation of his Secret Service detail, had been shaking hands and taking pictures with groups of Returned Peace Corps Volunteers. Luke and Kathryn had happened to be in the right place at the right time and had their picture taken with both the President and his wife. The Celebration had gone on for hours and had ended with an open air dance that created a gala atmosphere and ambiance to remember for the rest of your life.

Luke and Kathryn had arranged to fly directly from Dulles International Airport in Washington, D.C. to Guatemala City so that they could visit their newest orphanage and meet with the recently hired Director. These orphanages and the programs surrounding them had become their own special social entrepreneur project and they used this as a teaching example in The Quantum Abundance Theory Workshop. Each orphanage they sponsored had a small Board of Directors and essentially ran itself. Several years before one of their attorneys and a CPA had shown them how they could sponsor each orphanage into their business and thus create a long term self sustaining income for the orphanages. They had completed all the paperwork for this most recent orphanage and now were set to finalize the process for transferring each month the necessary monies into the orphanage account in Guatemala.

Years before, as they saw the challenges created for the local administrative personnel, Luke and Kathryn had reserved a position on each Board for one of them to fill and serve to help and relieve some of that stress of developing a new project. The orphanage they were on their way to this afternoon would eventually accommodate sixty-five children and would provide not only living quarters but an early preschool learning program and a strong recreational opportunity for all the children.

One interesting side effect which had occurred with two of the orphanages was that in the local villages that were home for the orphanages it had quickly become evident there was a need to increase the income of several local families. By forming a small local "cooperative" in each town Luke and Cesar had been able, over about an eighteen month period, to help them build their own cash flow through developing their own small businesses using the model Luke and Kathryn had designed for funding the orphanages themselves. Because helping local villagers increase their income had always been one part of Luke's past Peace Corps activities he felt a very special sense of achievement in helping these particular families.

As Luke looked around the large 757 aircraft that they were flying in toward Guatemala City he chuckled to himself. When the Guatemala I group had flown from Houston, Texas to Guatemala City in 1963 they had flown on Pan American World Airways. The old Pan American that had flown all over the world in the sixties no longer even existed. All of life is a constant change. Nothing remains the same.

Their approach into Guatemala City was beautiful, as always. The mountains were majestic in appearance and the varying shades of green foliage always enhanced the tropical feeling that came with being closer to the Equator.

After they quickly cleared Customs, Luke's old friend, Cesar, met them to take them to a hotel and then eventually on to the orphanage. Luke and Cesar had worked so well together years before in creating the clinic that when it came time to develop their first orphanage it had been a natural thing for Luke to locate him and ask him to serve on the Board of Directors. Today Cesar not only still served on two of the local Boards but also held a position on the Board of Cuerpo de Paz de los Niño's and had developed his own large international Wellness Marketing business. Cesar's wife, whom he had married shortly after Luke had completed his Peace Corps service, had died suddenly two years before and all of the extra activity and responsibility had helped Cesar ease through that difficult transition.

The three days that Luke and Kathryn had set aside for their visit were totally consumed with meetings, a full day tour of the new orphanage itself and what seemed to be an endless chain of obligations to be completed with the local government. They had dinner one evening with two Peace Corps Volunteers Cesar knew and it had been an enjoyable experience sharing with them the

Peace Corps of fifty years before, the exciting Fiftieth Anniversary Celebration and learning about the projects that the new Volunteers were involved with now in Guatemala.

One incident stood out for Luke on the second day of their visit. He and Cesar had walked about a half hour into the jungle that came right up to the very edge of the orphanage grounds. They had followed a fairly decent path for a few minutes and then had turned off the path in hopes perhaps of sighting some monkeys that stayed around the local area. As they stopped under the tall rising trees and allowed their eyes to become more adjusted to the shadows that often make up a part of the jungle cover Cesar reached across and touched Luke's arm as he pointed up and away from them. At first Luke did not see anything unusual. Then, as he carefully focused on tree limb after tree limb he saw a curving green stick hanging from one branch. No! It was not a stick at all! Atop the limb sat a bright green parrot like bird with a red breast! A Quetzal was quietly looking down at them as though he accepted that they belonged there as much as he did. That single, silent Quetzal seemed to approve of the growth and development that Luke, Kathryn and Cesar had been able to bring in their own quiet way to children in Guatemala. Luke knew how seldom the Quetzal is seen in the wild and as they slowly turned to retrace their steps he wished that Kathryn could have been with them to see the national bird of Guatemala.

In the late afternoon of their final day, as their airplane had risen into the air and flown out between the mountains heading Northwest toward Los Angeles and their change of planes that would take them home to Portland, they had reviewed all the activities of the past two weeks. They had seen old friends, they had met even more new ones and they remembered fifty years of world history. They had both leaned back in their seats and simply held hands for an extended period of time.

Finally Kathryn had leaned over and with her lips brushing Luke's ear had whispered. "Luke, I am very proud of you and all those people back there. I love you for what you give back to other people. I know that God truly has guided us in this endeavor. How did we ever become so blessed?"

GROUP DISCUSSION AIDS

It was suggested to us early in the development of this book that even though **WHAT DO I DO NOW?** is a novel we had included in it enough "life philosophy" that we should develop discussion suggestions for each chapter. We felt that rather than break the flow of the story we would place these discussion suggestions at the end of the book. These thoughts are not meant to limit discussion but rather to serve as thoughts around which group discussion will hopefully develop and advance on to much broader interaction.

CHAPTER ONE

1) Do you presently volunteer for any activities in your community?

2) What have you done in your life that has made a contribution to society around you?

3) How important is it to you to take time for prayer and meditation?

4) Do you have a "getaway" that you go to for recreation and retreat? How do you use it? Is it a restful retreat? A room? A garden? Does it bring you to a calm place in your life?

5) Some people crave solitude. Many fear it. How do you feel? Can you discuss these feelings?

CHAPTER TWO

1) What do you believe are your natural talents or skills? Do you make use of these in your daily life? How important to you is the relationship of those natural skills or talents to how you create, on a daily basis, your income and lifestyle?

2) How important in your life is the history of your ancestral heritage? Do you refer to it often in your daily life? What could you do right now that would enhance your life through a stronger relationship to your family's past?

2) Have you had the opportunity to travel broadly? If so, has this broadened your horizons and your personal lifestyle? How?

CHAPTER THREE

1) Have you ever visualized in a dream or pictured in your mind something that happened later in your life? Was it exactly the same? Were the details the same or only vaguely familiar?

2) If you are married or have a life partner, how did you meet? What special importance did how you met have to do with the development of your relationship?

3) Kathryn remembered her hometown of Ridgewood, New Jersey with warmth and fondness. How do you remember the town you grew up in? Do you still live in the same town in which you went to school and grew up?

4) Do you openly share with other people what it is you intend to accomplish with your life? If not, why do you keep those thoughts to yourself?

5) What can a "chance" encounter mean in your life? How do you think a person can best take advantage of those encounters?

CHAPTER FOUR

1) Have you ever been "downsized" in your employment? How did it feel? How did it happen? Are you still recovering from that event?

2) How did your job loss or change affect your family life? How did it affect your relationships with your friends?

3) What affect did your change in employment have on your relationship with your spouse or partner?

4) Did you feel a loss of personal identity by having a change in your employment? Is your profession or work activity your identity?

5) Have you felt a change in your personal self-esteem because of a change in your job, profession or employment?

6) Is your present career exciting and stimulating to you? Is it fun? How did you determine your present career? Did it determine itself for you through the need to earn an income as an adult?

1) Have you ever participated in a group such as the one at Luke's church? Was it valuable for you? In what ways can you describe it for this group you are with now?

2) Have you ever read the book, THINK AND GROW RICH? Did it have an impact on your personal growth and development? If yes, can you describe for the group what you felt it's value was to you?

3) Have you in the past ever had a person who was a mentor for you? Do you mentor anyone in your life right now? How might you go about helping to develop a mentoring project?

4) Luke had never developed a Life Purpose Statement. Do you feel this is an important step in a person's personal growth in life? If you have developed one, can you state your own Life Purpose Statement?

5) Have you ever truly assessed your own natural talents to help "determine what you might do with your life?" The majority of people do not guide their lives; their lives guide them. Do you agree or disagree with that statement?

6) Has there been a time in your life when you felt that God was not present with you because of a life situation relating to finances or your career? Does a question like this not even seem realistic to you?

7) Have you ever felt smarter than your employer or boss and wondered why you work for someone else? Can you openly discuss this with the group?

8) Does the idea of being your own boss or being self-employed frighten you? Does it bewilder you? Does it excite you?

CHAPTER SIX

1) Have you ever asked yourself, "How much is really enough?" What were you measuring or referring to? Income? Toys? Have you and your spouse/partner discussed this question?

2) Have you always been the principle provider in your family? What does that mean to you and to the others in your family?

3) How important to you is the use of self-help and/or motivational type books, CDs or DVDs? Do you use them regularly or not? Can you discuss why you do or do not use them?

4) Read the quotation by Jim Rohn at the beginning of Chapter Six. What special skills and talents does it take to develop this type discipline?

CHAPTER SEVEN

1) Luke had worked with Tom Simon for several years. After Simon's death Luke finally realized how big a man Simon had been. Do you have anyone in your life like Tom Simon?

2) Describe in written form at least two people you are aware of who are like Tom Simon. Discuss with the group what makes these people different and special.

3) Read the Carnegie quotation at the first of Chapter Seven. Do you agree, disagree or have no opinion on the statement. Can you discuss why you feel the way you do?

CHAPTER EIGHT

1) Do you regularly set goals for your life activities? Do you feel goal setting is important in attaining success and happiness? Can you discuss this with the group?

2) Have you ever thought very much about how and why people, books and coincidental events appear and occur in your life? Is this difficult for you to discuss?

3) If you are single how do you make decisions like the one facing Luke in Chapter Eight?

4) If you are married is the process different than for a single person? Describe and discuss the differences or similarities.

5) In your childhood family how were major decisions made? Were they made by your Father, as the Head of the House? By your Mother? As a family? Have you carried your childhood family's decision making processes forward into your own life?

CHAPTER NINE

Some of the reviewers of **WHAT DO I DO NOW?** said they felt this was the most important chapter in the book. In this chapter Tom Simon presents the Three Boxes that he feels people fall into socially and economically.

1) Do you agree or disagree with Tom Simon that people are in one of the Three Boxes? Can you discuss what this means to you? Do these Boxes make you think about your own life? Would you rather not think about your life this way?

2) Does The Principle of Tithing make sense to you? Why or why not?

3) Do you agree or disagree with The Principle of Delayed Gratification? Can you discuss your thoughts with the group?

4) Do you presently have a residual income source? If your answer is yes, discuss how this affects your decision making. If your answer is no, what would it mean to your lifestyle if you did have a residual income stream?

5) In his booklet titled "Changing Your Box" Tom Simon stresses that to achieve Abundance, people need to be moving toward Box Number Three. Thinking to yourself (not openly with the group) which Box are you in today? Where would you like to be? What will it take to get there? What parts of this can you discuss openly with the group?

CHAPTER TEN

1) What is required for you to be able to "step out on your own new road" as Kathryn says and rely on faith for your success?

2) Almost everyone has faith in something. Can you express what you have faith in? What does that expression mean to you personally?

3) Paul Zane Pilzer is a world recognized economist and author. Can you rephrase his quotation at the beginning of Chapter Ten and discuss its importance with the group?

CHAPTER ELEVEN

1) Can you define the word "entrepreneur"? Discuss with your group what it takes to be an entrepreneur.

2) Do you plan your days, weeks, and months with care? Or do they just seem to float by?

3) There is a new term being used in business. It is "social entrepreneur." Do you know what that term means? Discuss what you think this business model means to the development of Third World countries.

4) Are you influenced through emotion, logic, visual impressions, sound or some other sense?

CHAPTER TWELVE

1) How important is your personal growth in relation to your employment or source of income?

2) Have you personally ever been the recipient of a "pay it forward" situation such as existed between Luke and Dave? What did that mean to you

3) How important to you are incentive trips and contests in comparison to your actual wage, salary or commissions?

4) Think of your childhood family. How was money regarded in the home? What were the spoken and unspoken thoughts or talk about money that influenced your life today? Discuss these thoughts with the group.

5) Are you subconsciously repeating the teachings of your childhood? Are these positive or negative?

CHAPTER THIRTEEN

1) Where do you enjoy going for vacation? Do you take regular vacations or do you stay close to home on most of your time off work?

2) Can you recall how a specific conversation such as the one between Luke and Albert influenced your life? Does this seem real to you or is it just a part of a fiction novel?

CHAPTER FOURTEEN

1) Have you ever studied the concept of visualization? Do you consciously use visualization in your own life? If so, why do you do it? Discuss the pros and cons of this concept with the group. Discuss with your group whether the people in the group think it works or not in real life.

2) How does visualization relate, or not relate, to your personal religious beliefs? Discuss this with the group.

CHAPTER FIFTEEN

1) Have you ever experienced what Kathryn refers to as, "A Moment of Grace?" Can you discuss that moment and what it meant?

2) Do you live in your "heart home?" If no, why not? What does that term mean to you?

3) Have you ever received a gift that has had lifelong importance to you? What was it? Can you discuss with your group its' importance and what that has meant to you?

EPILOGUE

1) Do you have abundant excess income that you are free to do with as you see fit and as you determine? That may be a question you do not want to discuss with a group. If not, can you discuss the importance of this issue to you in your personal life?

2) Most people are obligated to pay bills with almost one hundred percent of their personal income. What would you do differently with your life, time and income if you were able to determine how and where to spend at least fifty percent of your monthly income?

3) Have you ever thought about the importance of "cash flow" in your life? What does "cash flow" mean to you? Discuss with the group the importance of "cash flow" in a business and in an individuals personal life.

4) Do you have a major charitable project or group that you support regularly? Discuss with the group the importance of charitable contributions.

5) Have you ever taken time to think about what you might be able to give back to your country? Discuss with the group what you think this thought really means and whether or not it is truly realistic.

6) Have you ever considered becoming a "social entrepreneur"? What could you do that would qualify you as a "social entrepreneur?"

NOTES AND BIBLIOGRAPHY

INTRODUCTION

For information about the Peace Corps go to: www.peacecorps.gov.

For information about Returned Peace Corps Volunteers go to: www.peacecorpsconnect.org.

For information about MannaRelief Ministries go to www.mannarelief.org.

For information about Foundation for International Community Assistance (FINCA) go to: www.finca.org.

CHAPTER ONE

Quote that begins Chapter One is from President Kennedy's First Inaugural Address, January 1961.

CHAPTER TWO

Frost, Robert, The Road Not Taken, Mountain Interval, New York, Henry Holt & Co., 1920

CHAPTER THREE

W. Clement Stone quote from Stove's Famous Quotes, Wikipedia, External Links, 2010.

CHAPTER FOUR

"Until you select....," Napoleon Hill. This famous quotation of Mr. Hill was used by him in many public speeches and in his audio training tapes and cassettes. For an excellent discussion by Mr. Hill of The Principle of The Definiteness of Purpose see Chapter Three, The Master Key To Riches, Napoleon Hill, Fawcett Crest Books, 1965.

"It is easier....," The New English Bible, New Testament, Mathew 19:24, Oxford University Press, Cambridge University Press, 1961.

"Go to now....," The Holy Bible, King James Version, Eyre and Spotswood Ltd., London

CHAPTER FIVE

Robert Kiyosaki and Sharon Lechter, <u>Rich Dad's The Business School</u>, Video Plus, Lake Dallas, Texas, 2005.

CHAPTER SIX

Rohn, Jim, <u>The Treasury of Quotes,</u> <u>Jim Rohn</u> International, Irving, Texas, 1994.

CHAPTER SEVEN

Carnegie, Andrew, (N.D.) BrainyQuote.com. Retrieved December 12, 2010 from BrainyQuote website:

www.brainyquote.com/quotes/a/andrewcarn133933.html.

CHAPTER EIGHT

Ralph Waldo Emerson, May 1803-April 1882. This statement is attributed to Ralph Waldo Emerson in numerous public domain quotations.

CHAPTER NINE

Thurgood Marshall, 1908-1993, BrainyQuote.com. Retrieved December 12, 2010 from BrainyQuote website:

www.brainyquote.com/quotes/m/thurgoodmarshall.

<u>The Holy Bible, New International Version</u>, Copyright 1973, 1978, 1984, International Bible Society, permission of Zondervan Bible Publishers.

CHAPTER TEN

Pilzer, Paul Zane, <u>The Wellness Revolution,</u> John Wiley and Sons, Inc., New York, 2002

CHAPTER ELEVEN

Jim Rohn, <u>The Treasury of Quotes,</u> Jim Rohn International, Irving, Texas, 1994.

CHAPTER TWELVE

The New Possibility Thinkers Bible, (King James Version), Robert Schuller, Executive Editor, Thomas Nelson Publishers, Nashville, 1996.

CHAPTER THIRTEEN

The Chinese proverb quoted here is ancient in both age and wisdom.

Information about media opportunities for developmentally disabled persons. www.mainstreamedmedia.org

Oregon Association of Minority Entrepreneurs www.oame.org

The National Association for Black Veterans, Inc. www.nabvetsportland.org

CHAPTER FOURTEEN

Murphy, Joseph, PhD, DD, LLD, The Power Of Your Subconscious Mind, Prentice-Hall, Inc., Englewood Cliffs, New Jersey, 1963.

Hill, Napoleon, Think and Grow Rich, Fawcett Crest, New York, 1960

Sam Caster quote used in speeches about Social Entrepreneurship and use authorized by Mr. Caster.

CHAPTER FIFTEEN

This quote by Kathleen Peters was first used in the workshop "Setting Goals in Your Business" 2000.

Bartlett, Elaine, A Handbook to Higher Truth, Spiritual Law, Product Code, EBO32010, OBVIOUS, retrieved from www.trysomethingobvious.com, 2011.

EPILOGUE

John Fitzgerald Kennedy, (1917-1963), This is a statement used by President Kennedy in more than one public speech.

ABOUT THE AUTHORS

Philip and Kathleen met through their involvement in the Wellness Marketing Industry. They were both single at the time with grown children. They recognized in the first moment of meeting that they would be spending the rest of their lives together. Their ensuing romance and devotion to each other is an amazing story in its own right. They have been asked a number of times to script it out for a book or film. Today they have, together, built a large Wellness Marketing Business that spans the globe.

"In the economy of the first decade of the Twenty-First Century it has become essential that people who truly wish to live comfortably and make a significant contribution to society must become entrepreneurs. To simply have a job and trade hours for dollars each week no longer meets the needs of most families," says Philip.

Born and raised in Oregon, Philip is a fifth generation Oregonian. He has owned a major herbal products company, a pharmaceutical laboratory and successfully owned and operated several farms over the past forty years. During this time he became the world's largest grower, producer and distributor of products made from the herb comfrey. He is known as an authority on the growing of comfrey and served as a consultant to Weyerhauser Co., Texaco and U.S. Steel. Philip has been an integral part of the growth of the Wellness Industry for over thirty years.

Kathleen was born into a Navy family in Virginia and in her teen years moved to New Jersey. She raised her family there and in her twenties was exposed to corporate community responsibility through XEROX. Kathleen served in several capacities with XEROX and after twenty years left that corporate life to join Philip in building their Wellness Marketing Business full-time.

Kathleen and Philip combined their families in 1998 giving them a total of five children. Together they have created and presented workshops and seminars worldwide in the areas of

Goal Setting and Development, Building Your Own Wellness Marketing Business and several motivational programs. They travel the globe in support of their own business and presenting specialized workshops upon request.

They truly are a bicoastal family, maintaining full-time homes in both New Jersey and Oregon.

Philip and Kathleen have brought together their diverse talents and backgrounds to make available through National Information Services Corporation a variety of publications, workshops and seminars in support of both Wellness Marketing and the growing field of Social Entrepreneurship.

For information about speaking engagements, training seminars and events go to www.whatdoidonow.biz.

YOU CAN
CHANGE YOUR LIFE!!

Learn More About:

- Wellness Marketing
- Residual Long Term Income
- Becoming a Social Entrepreneur
- The Quantum Abundance Theory
- The Fortune Formula

at www.netwellbeing.com/peters

To Order Additional Copies Of **NOW WHAT DO I DO?** Send $16.95 + $3.00 ($19.95) for shipping and handling to

National Information Services Corporation
PO Box 45
Canby, Oregon 97013
USA

For More Information:
www.thepetersgroup.biz
(503) 682-1851
info@thepetersgroup.biz